RE-APPRAISAL
of
REGIONAL
POLICIES
in
OECD
COUNTRIES

ORGANISATION FOR ECONOMIC CO-OPERATION AND DEVELOPMENT

PARIS 1974

The Organisation for Economic Co-operation and Development (OECD) was set up under a Convention signed in Paris on 14th December, 1960, which provides that the OECD shall promote policies designed :

— to achieve the highest sustainable economic growth and employment and a rising standard of living in Member countries, while maintaining financial stability, and thus to contribute to the development of the world economy;

— to contribute to sound economic expansion in Member as well as non-member countries in the process of economic development;

— to contribute to the expansion of world trade on a multilateral, non-discriminatory basis in accordance with international obligations.

The Members of OECD are Australia, Austria, Belgium, Canada, Denmark, Finland, France, the Federal Republic of Germany, Greece, Iceland, Ireland, Italy, Japan, Luxembourg, the Netherlands, New Zealand, Norway, Portugal, Spain, Sweden, Switzerland, Turkey, the United Kingdom and the United States.

*
* *

PREFACE

In recent years regional policies and their relationship to national economic and social policies have attracted increasing governmental and public attention.

With a view to assisting Member Governments in their continuing task of reviewing and modifying their regional policies and to assisting public understanding of the issues involved, the Organisation entrusted the responsible Working Party of the Industry Committee with re-assessing the role, objectives and application of such policies.

The present report is based on the Working Party's consideration over a number of years of the general issues and on its analysis of the impact on Member countries of particular problems and the policies pursued in meeting those problems. It reflects as accurately as possible the general views of the Working Party as a whole without necessarily each and every point reflecting the views of each of its members.

TABLE OF CONTENTS

I

INTRODUCTION

Almost all OECD countries now pursue regional policies of one kind or another* and it is safe to assert that they are likely to do so for as far ahead as can be foreseen. In some they have been in existence for a very long time, in others they are of more recent inception. It has been part of the continuing work of the OECD to exchange information on these policies between the Members and to attempt to draw such lessons from experience as can be usefully applied to the formulation of policies in the future. The aim of this report is to survey what has been learned from this exchange and bring to the attention of Member Governments the more important conclusions which have emerged from joint study. In carrying out its study the Working Party has not only attempted to absorb a vast amount of official information supplied by the Member Governments but over the years has carried out on the spot investigations in several countries, France, the United Kingdom, United States, Italy, Japan, Spain and Austria. The OECD has also commissioned a special study by the former Chairman of the Working Party which was published in 1973. **

Reasons for Study

A study of this kind must be practical in purpose, to discover not only the merits but also the defects of existing policies, so that what is good in them can be further utilized and what has proved unsuccessful or ineffective can be discarded. Experience has in fact suggested that there are elements of good and bad, of effective and ineffective and of worth-while and not so worth-while in the policies that have been

---

*   See: The Regional Factor in Economic Development, OECD, Paris, 1970.
**   Issues of Regional Policy. Report by A. Emanuel, OECD, Paris, 1973.

pursued. Only by appraising the policies in a critical rather than a complacent spirit can the full benefit of a practical study be obtained.

There are other more specific reasons why policies should be critically appraised.

1) In most countries that have been studied they represent an attempt to deal with continuing and long-term problems. Since the problems will not disappear in the short run an adequate appraisal should be of lasting rather than passing value.

2) The problems are often substantial and require a substantial effort to tackle them effectively. If regional policies are to be compatible with the general objective of securing national growth any failings or weaknesses in them should be identified and corrected.

3) Regional policies can sometimes conflict with other, equally desirable, objectives of Government. Recognition that there can be conflicts of objectives, as, for example, between national growth and the elimination of regional disparities* is a first step towards reconciling objectives and apportioning resources between them.

4) In a changing world new sources of regional disequilibria are always at work and the goals of regional policy may change and become more ambitious. It cannot therefore be expected that regional problems will in general be overcome** but there is a continuing need to review the reasons for success and failure and to consider whether changed policies would produce better results.

5) Regional policies have not only been in continual evolution but have widened in scope and scale. In consequence, the problems of definition of objectives, selection of methods, allocation and use of resources and organisation have become much more complex. The need is therefore enhanced to consider the implication for policy of this growing complexity.

6) In recent years it has become increasingly apparent that regional policies in individual countries have an impact beyond their

---

* The conflict between growth and regional policies is referred to in the Growth of Output, 1960-1980, OECD, Paris, 1970.

** Idem p. 137. This has also been borne out by later studies of the Working Party. In the United Kingdom, in which perhaps the largest and most sustained effort to deal with regional problems has taken place, the judgment of the Government is summed up as follows: "The ending of regional imbalance has been an objective of successive Governments in the United Kingdom for nearly four decades. Much has been achieved but no solution is yet in sight". Cmnd. 4942, HMSO, March 1972.

frontiers and that they not only offer scope for co-operation but also for conflict between nations. * It is appropriate, therefore, for an international body such as the OECD to give particular attention to those aspects of regional policy which are of mutual concern to its Members.

Critical Issues

The above list, which is by no means exhaustive, provides sufficient reason for the kind of study which has been undertaken. To this, however, may be added another set of considerations. It is often said, and it is true, that regional policies are largely experimental. The frequency and in some cases rapidity with which they change (and sometimes thereby lose effect even if temporarily) is evidence of this. They are, however, not only experimental but also controversial. In few countries is there any consensus view over the whole range of regional policies, comprising various objectives and methods. Though controversy is the life blood of democracy it is sterile if it does not lead in the end to acceptance of certain lessons from experience, objectively assessed. In regional policies, as in other matters, there are legitimate grounds for differences of view and controversy over the whole field, whether of aims and objectives or policies and methods. There is obviously no more possibility within an organisation such as the OECD to reach a complete consensus of view than there is in individual countries.

What can be done is to establish those matters on which there is substantial agreement and those on which all that can be said is something on both sides - that there are advantages and disadvantages in certain policies of which account should be taken by the responsible authorities in formulating their policies. This is the approach adopted in this report. It leads perforce to greater concentration on this latter category, the controversial issues, for they are the ones about which discussion is most likely to be needed. The former category consists largely of 'ultimate' objectives on which most people, and their Governments, tend to be agreed just because they are 'ultimate' and are not yet processed into the stage at which difficult choices and decisions have to be made. ** There is not much disagreement about the need or objective of higher standards of living for all, for bringing into use of unemployed resources, for limiting growth where congestion or social costs can reduce average productivity, for greater equality of opportunity or for lessening the disparities between different regions, for environmental improvement and eliminating congestion, over-crowding, poor housing and other social hardships. Where the

---

*   See Issues of Regional Policy, Ch. XI.
**   See Issues of Regional Policy, Ch. II.

disagreement begins is on the policies and methods by which laudable aims should be achieved and how the costs involved should be borne by different elements of the community.

A number of critical issues of regional policies have been identified all of which, in greater or lesser degree, and to a different extent in different countries, are also controversial. In summary they comprise such questions as:

1) The nature, causes and scale of regional problems in a given national setting.

2) The criteria that should determine the choice of policies and methods including the allocation of resources to deal with them.

3) The relation of regional to the other problems that confront Governments, such as national development and economic growth, physical planning, social progress and the protection of the environment.

4) The efficacy of alternative approaches to the solution of regional problems in a changing world, and the evaluation of regional policies in terms of costs and benefits.

5) The institutional and organisational framework required to deal with regional problems.

6) The bearing of international considerations on regional policies.

It is as well to state here at the outset that none of these general issues present themselves in the same way or with the same emphasis, in all countries. The countries of the OECD range from the very large to the very small, in area, population and resources. They differ greatly in economic structure, in stage of development and dynamic forces at work, in degree of urbanism, and in political and social organisation. What is significant, however, is that, despite these great differences, regional problems and policies give rise to issues in which there are many elements of similarity, so that the process of comparison and contrast throws up lessons and principles which have some degree of common applicability in most of the countries. The real differences between countries have not therefore been seen as grounds for giving up all attempts to seek a common framework of discussion of regional problems but only as a factor that must at all times be borne in mind.

The broad questions or issues which have been listed above present themselves in most countries, despite the major differences between them. Within their general framework questions of a more detailed nature also arise, to which, of course, the answers vary from country to country. Such derivative questions will be specific to the particular conditions of each country and cannot be answered except on the basis of detailed investigation and knowledge of all the relevant circumstances. Essentially, this can only be done by Governments themselves in the light of the political and value judgments which are accepted in their countries. It is not therefore the aim of this report to make judgments on the validity or otherwise of the policies pursued by individual Governments or of the solutions they adopt to the problems which are specific to them.

The derivative questions which flow from the broader issues are too numerous to be given in detail in an introduction. They include the meaning and measurement of "regional disparities" or "imbalances"; the advantages and disadvantages of alternative policies such as "work to the workers" or "workers to the work"; the impact of policies on regional imbalances and national growth; the usefulness of incentives and restraints; the interdependence of regions; the preparation of "strategies" for regional development; the influence of changes in industrial structure on the choice of policies; decentralization and growth point policies; the financial resource-use aspect of policies and the problems of coordination and control.

Structure of the Report

Such a list, which is not exhaustive, indicates the wide range of topics which would be involved in a comprehensive examination of regional issues. The topics are interrelated, so that separate discussion of each would inevitably involve overlapping and repetition of argument and factual material. This consideration and the desirability of avoiding excessive length have determined the structure of the report.

It begins (Ch. II) with a brief and largely descriptive account of the nature of regional problems as they have presented themselves in the countries studied by the Working Party, then proceeds to a discussion of the central issue of "regional balance" as an objective of policy, and of the bearing of national factors and change on regional situations (Ch's III and IV). The next two chapters consider the questions arising from the need for regional strategies and from the variety of instruments and methods used in regional policies. Ch. VII discusses the issues involved for public finance, planning, coordination and administration and Ch. VIII considers the subject in terms of its international aspects. The aim of the concluding Chapter (IX) is not to provide a summary but to draw attention to the main general points which emerge from the report taken as a whole.

II

THE NATURE OF REGIONAL PROBLEMS

Any evaluation of regional policies and the methods which go with them poses the question: what are they about? In other words, what is the nature of the problem or problems for which special policies appear to be required? The studies of the Working Party have shown that there is no single concept of "the regional problems" which uniformly fits the circumstances of all countries. They have also shown that in most countries regional policy is concerned with a multiplicity of problems. It is important that this should be realized from the outset since much confusion results from attempts to apply single and common categories and concepts to widely differing situations. A brief survey of some of the salient features in various countries will illustrate these points. *

In the three countries in which regional policies have been longest established and most prominent, namely the United Kingdom, France and Italy, the differences between them are at least as significant as the similarities. In each of them attention tends to be focussed on the problem of regional "imbalances" or "disparities" but these terms do no more than provide a common vocabulary for what are, in practice, very different problems with different origins. Each country has its special "problem areas" or regions.

United Kingdom

Thus, in the United Kingdom, the problem areas are largely those mainly peripheral regions of Scotland, the North of England and South Wales, which were heavily industrialized during the Industrial Revolution.

---

* A fuller description of regional problems and policies is to be given in an accompanying report.

Basic industries such as coal, iron and steel, shipbuilding and textiles developed in these regions rather than elsewhere as a result of favourable technical conditions, mainly the presence of raw materials but also even favourable climate. In recent decades, as a result of a combination of circumstances, the rise of competitive industries elsewhere and changes in technologies which diminished manpower needs and the rise of new modern industries with different locational requirements, these became regions of industrial decline rather than expansion in employment terms. In terms also of relative importance in the national economy, other regions, notably the South East and Midlands, became the expanding regions. The regional imbalance in the United Kingdom was therefore essentially a reflection of the changes in the structure of the national economy. There are also special problems in Northern Ireland.

In comparative terms, the United Kingdom has been an advanced, highly developed industrialized country for a century and a half. It has remained a growing economy, even if its growth rate in recent decades has been lower than that of countries which have more recently become industrialized. The very elements which have conditioned its growth have, however, been the same factors which have influenced its regional structure and created the imbalances which are now seen as a major problem for regional policy.

The nature and scale of the regional imbalances are also sui generis. The "declining regions" by no means present a picture of unrelieved stagnation. While unemployment rates have been persistently higher than the average of the country as a whole, often twice as high, considerable restructuring of industry has in fact taken place. This, coupled with some outward migration, has meant that the great bulk of the workforce, something like 95% on average, has remained in employment. Incomes and activity rates have tended to be lower than elsewhere but not drastically different. In other respects, housing, environment and social welfare, conditions are not significantly or uniformly worse than elsewhere in the country except in the older industrial and mining areas which have suffered particularly from derelection - a legacy of the Industrial Revolution. Such problems exist elsewhere, in the "intermediate" and other regions. Nor are standards of living uniformly worse in the problem regions than else-where, since in the so-called "more prosperous" regions, higher incomes and employment opportunities are to some extent offset by higher living costs and housing shortages leading to overcrowding. Social problems of poverty and distress in fact exist in many of the large cities and urban areas, in "prosperous" and "less prosperous" regions alike.

The United Kingdom is, of course, a highly urbanized country with 40% of the population living in cities whose populations exceed 100,000 and with almost one third of the whole population concentrated in the South-East region and one-seventh in the area of the capital. There is thus not only an economic imbalance but one of population distribution and land use and availability. The regional imbalance problem is thus not only an economic one, of unemployment and other economic disparities, but also a physical one, of great variations in size and densities and economic functions and structures of urban communities. The problem of ensuring that economic growth and change takes place in accordance with the physical capabilities of cities and environmental conditions constitutes an important element in the "regional problem" of the country as a whole. The physical problems are clearly not confined to the regions with relatively high unemployment. They exist in all regions and exercise an inescapable influence on the allocation of resources for development of all kinds, including communications, energy and social services.

Neither regional policies, extending over four decades, nor the restructuring of industry or emigration, have noticeably altered the imbalances, particularly in unemployment. Unemployment rates have remained persistently higher in the peripheral regions than in the country as a whole. In absolute terms there has undoubtedly been considerable progress but in relative terms the imbalance has remained virtually unchanged.

Italy

As in the United Kingdom, the "problem" regions of Italy constitute a very large part of the country. The "Mezzogiorno" or South has roughly 40% of the population and the problem areas as a whole constitute more than half the country's population. In each country the "regional problem" lies in the economic disparities or imbalance between the problem regions and the rest but beyond this the differences are more significant than the similarities. The degree of disparity is much greater in Italy than the United Kingdom. In terms of average incomes per head, differences in the latter are marginal. In Italy, however, they are very large indeed. In the Mezzogiorno, it was about 62% in 1972 of the national average (virtually unchanged over the last twenty years although there has been substantial progress in the improvement of production structures and in the absolute and per capita level of return) and around 40% of that of the North West. * The problem of

* These are only average figures and they mask the great differences within the Mezzogiorno itself and the existence of areas of extreme poverty which have received little benefit from the policies affecting the zones of development.

15

Southern Italy has not been one of decline of industrially developed areas, as in the United Kingdom, but of initial backwardness and poverty, accentuated by rapidly growing populations and the decline of agriculture as a source of employment leading to massive emigration, without which the problem of poverty would presumably have been even more severe, but which also represents a drain of the more active age-groups. Since the initiation of a positive regional policy aimed at promoting the economic growth of the Mezzogiorno, there has been progress in industrialization and in income levels. The industrial heart of Italy is, however, in the North and this too has expanded. To some extent new industrial growth has been offset in Southern Italy by the decline of some established industries facing increased competition from the North. In short, up to a certain point, recent industrial development in the south of Italy has had as the counterpart the decline of certain industries which are predominantly of pre-capitalistic character. Moreover, the relatively high growth rate of the Italian economy has not lessened the scale of regional disparities.

While the problems of the Mezzogiorno are the most acute and tend to receive most attention in discussions of regional policy in Italy, other regions also pose problems and these include parts of the centre and the North. There are significant disparities between the North-West on the one hand and the central and North-Eastern regions on the other. The rapid industrial growth in the major northern cities, accompanied by large inward immigration from the South, has posed problems of urban congestion, overcrowding and social welfare. In each region the need has existed for greater investment infrastructure and general development, requiring a co-ordinated approach to the development of the country as a whole. Recognition that all regions have their special problems and that national policies and planning must take account of these finds expression in the wide approach to national economic planning as embodied, for example, in the National Economic Plan for 1960-1970.

The rapid overall development of the Italian national economy in the last decade or so has therefore accentuated the need to see the regional problem of Italy, not as that of any single region or group of regions but as that of the part that all regions should play in the national framework. Within this concept the need for overcoming the special disabilities of the Mezzogiorno becomes part of the national economic planning process aimed at a greater utilization of the resources of the country, in land and manpower, reducing excessive concentration in certain other parts of the country and expanding and diversifying the entire, especially industrial, economic base.

16

France

In France, the concept of "imbalance" is, as in the other two countries, a central feature of the overall "regional problem" but the nature of the imbalances is different, resulting in a different approach to regional policy. In the post-war years France has been a country of rapid economic change and development, characterized by decline of employment in some basic industries such as agriculture and coal, and the development of many modern industries. These changes have been accompanied by considerable internal migration such that it is estimated that 28% of the population changed the region of residence between 1962 and 1968. * No single statistical indicator, such as unemployment or income levels, provides an adequate picture of the disparities between the 22 regions into which the country is divided. Since each region has its own and different balance of economic opportunity, there are considerable variations in population densities, employment and activity rates, incomes, housing and living standards generally. To analyse regional disparities in terms of the "dualistic" pattern between North and South, or in terms of single criteria such as unemployment or low incomes would not adequately describe the problem of regional imbalance as it exists in France.

The regional problem is perhaps more correctly defined as that of adapting the regions of France to the changes brought about by the development of the national economy, involving the run down of some industries and the expansion of others, inevitably resulting in differential rates of growth in different regions. It is therefore not so much a question of "rectifying" imbalances or regional disparities to bring about a theoretical evenness of development in all regions or of "closing the gaps" between more and less developed regions as of the positive development of France as a whole in ways which take account of the needs and potentialities of the regions. Such an approach involves the concept of "aménagement du territoire" in which the development of the country as a whole is conceived not only in global, macro-economic terms but in terms of all its regions and of the "balance" between them. The concept is a dynamic one and does not necessarily lead to a uniform rate of development or attainment of common standards to each separate part of the country. The way in which the concept is applied is to be found in the successive National Plans in which the regional component is an integral part.

Within this general concept different regions or groups of regions present different problems, all of which have to be allowed for in the

_____

* See "Statistiques et Indicateurs des Régions Françaises", INSEE. Paris (annual publication), for comprehensive comparisons between regions.

policy of "aménagement du territoire". The foremost of these problems is the concentration of population and economic activity in the Paris region, with over a fifth of the economically active population, with a considerably higher growth rate than that of the country as a whole. The problems of urban congestion in all forms have made it virtually a national necessity to seek to restrain the growth of Paris and to foster compensatory growth elsewhere, so far as this can be done without weakening the economic life of the country of which Paris is clearly a mainstay.

The Paris region is not the only "growth" region. The rapid rate of growth in the South East corner poses problems of infrastructure development and the location of development to avoid excessive urban concentration. By contrast, regions within the West and South-West and the massif central require development to offset the effects of modernization of agriculture and rural decline while in the North and East the decline of the traditional heavy industries call for conversion of their industrial structures.

The regional problem, it will be seen, divides broadly into two main aspects, to reduce the centralization of economic life in the Paris region or to secure a better balance between that region and the provinces; and to foster development in the other regions in accordance with their special problems. The problem is, however, set in a framework of growing population and of disparate economic growth potential as between regions.

France is also a large country with a relatively low overall density of population. There can be no question of each and every single part of every town, village and rural area progressing in the same degree or reaching the same standard levels of economic life. Differential growth is unavoidable and the problem of regional balance is that of finding sufficient growth opportunities within each region for the populations that are expected to remain within them after allowing for such internal migration as is socially acceptable. The continuing urbanization of France and the growth of service industries provide both a need and an opportunity for selective growth in "métropoles d'équilibre" or "counterbalancing capitals" and new industrial areas conveniently located within other regions.

In such a situation it is not practicable or sensible to regard regional economic growth and regional physical planning as separate elements but as different aspects of the single problem of how best to shape the future development of France as a whole. The regional problem is not that of remedying disparities or securing a fixed and predetermined pattern of growth but to ensure a satisfactory balance of development between the regions, inevitably allowing for their diverse character. Unlike Italy and the United Kingdom, therefore, the key "regional problem" is not that of the imbalance between 40-50% of the country and the rest but of the inter-regional balance of the whole country.

It automatically implies a collection of policies, in economic development, infrastructure investment and social services requiring assessment of the competing claims of the regions on the resources available, and decisions on the allocations of resources, and their phasing and priorities between the competing claims. It calls therefore for an apparatus of decision making, in relation to the central problem of objectives and priorities as between regions and the local problems of the nature and pace of development within regions.

Each of these three countries can be regarded as a locus classicus of the "regional problem" and are countries in which strong regional policies are of long standing. But the foregoing description serves to show that there is no common formula which fits them all. Examples drawn from other countries reinforce the conclusion that it is as important to recognize the individual nature of the regional problems of each country as to find general similarities between them. The Working Party has not found that any simple system of classification fits the circumstances of individual countries and this survey of what constitutes regional problems continues by reference to individual countries or geographical groups.

Nordic Countries

The term "imbalance" can also be used to describe the regional problems of four Nordic countries, but the differences in geographical configuration, size and distances, location, resources, economic structure, population distribution and urban growth, as well as the influence of change, preclude simple generalizations. The imbalances in each of them are not static but reflect the changes in underlying economic forces, from the modernization and increasing scale of some primary industries to the development of new secondary and tertiary industries and occupations which, against a background of improved communications and transport systems, favour some locations rather than others.

All of these countries as a whole have been economically progressive and prosperous but the improvements in conditions have not been evenly spread since the differing advantages and disadvantages of particular regions and local areas act to favour some locations rather than others. The regional problem is therefore not that of a simple contrast between "backward" or declining regions on the one hand and the more advanced and progressive regions on the other but more that of geographical shifts, interregionally and within regions of the location of economic activity. These shifts are usually accompanied by a diminished role of the smaller centres and an increase in the size of those towns which provide a focal or nodal point for development of central services for themselves and the surrounding regions.

In each of the four countries there is heavy centralization of population and advanced economic activity in the capital regions, roughly, 25% in Denmark, Norway and Finland and a similar proportion in Sweden, including the area facing Denmark. Though none of these cities are large by world standards, ranging roughly from half to one million population, they are very large in proportional terms. Given the strength of centripetal forces in the modern world, the problem of regional balance is that of ensuring that other parts of the country share in the general economic progress and that the pattern of human settlement in other parts is adapted to the requisite conditions for economic growth. The problem of regional balance extends therefore to the organisation of the country as a whole and requires attention to be focussed especially on regions or local areas which, whether because of remoteness or scattered populations, require special support if a desirable regional balance is to be achieved in the country as a whole.

None of this necessarily presupposes an attempt to maintain rigidly the existing pattern of population settlement irrespective of the economic capabilities of different regions and locations. Since not all localities are equally well placed, the problem for policy makers is to identify those which are most likely to serve as focal points for the development which is necessary to ensure that the country as a whole retains a satisfactory balance between its regions.

Benelux

The Benelux countries, i. e. Belgium, the Grand Duchy of Luxembourg and the Netherlands, like other European countries, are experiencing some regional imbalance, resulting from the economic rundown, in various regions, of traditional industries in decline or highly static, as well as from growth in other regions due to the advent of new industries or the development of industries belonging to steadily expanding sectors. As in most other countries geographical imbalance in distribution of economic activity has been a normal feature of the structure of each country but the imbalances have changed throughout the post-war period as population growth, reconstruction and overall industrial growth have been accompanied by sectoral change, in particular the run down of such industries as coal and agriculture as a source of employment. Sectoral change has been accompanied by migration to the growing areas and relative stagnation or decline in others. This is a continuing situation and the regional problem cannot be considered just in terms of a static contrast between well defined regions or disparities in employment and income but of a fluid situation in which constant development brings about shifts in the location of population and industrial life, and certain adjustments, whether or not combined with population movements. Another feature is the high density of populations, the tendencies to concentration in the large cities such as the Randstadt area, Brussels and Antwerp, and the relative decline of rural areas, tendencies enhanced by the development of communications, the small distances between main centres and the rise of service industries generally.

The aims of regional policy have themselves tended to evolve in keeping with the changes in the actual situation. For example, the areas for which special support measures are provided have changed. In the Netherlands, a country of limited area with a high population density, a key regional problem is that of the future distribution of people over the whole country. This problem, together with that of the continuing unsatisfactory employment situation in the northern part of the country, both qualitatively and quantitatively, led the Government in 1971 to decide on the setting up of an overall structure plan (OSP) for the region. The central question around which the OSP is to be drawn up is that of the place of the North in the national economy and in which way the region can perform its economic and social functions in an optimal way within the limits of the possibilities of the national economy. South Limburg, whose situation has been strongly affected by the closure of coal mines, is another region which requires a continuous active regional policy. The labour market in this area, which is a frontier region bordering on Belgium and Germany, has been seriously perturbed in recent years by the increase in the number of people commuting to work in Germany. This phenomenon has led to a slackening in the rate of re-industrialization which is needed to compensate for the job losses consequent on the closure of the coal mines.

The regional problem in Belgium undoubtedly stems from certain general problems, which can be roughly classified in two groups. The first consists of the difficulties inherent in the old-established basic industries, especially the coal and textile sectors, with all their implications for the minor processing industries dependent on them, and for the tertiary sector. The second group arises from the relative under-industrialization of certain parts of the country, some of which were and are distinguished by a surplus of productive labour;

in other words, a relatively high level of population. These two
significant groups of problems are aggravated by another factor of
regional disparity, whose impact has been and still is a source of
anxiety: the economic development of such towns as Brussels and
Antwerp, with the resulting repercussions on migration flows to these
areas of rapid growth. Again, for many decades, a number of Belgian
frontier regions have given rise to problems of adjustment: the areas
adjacent to France, the Netherlands, Germany and the Grand Duchy
of Luxembourg. Notwithstanding the creation of the European Economic
Community, the fact that the frontier exists continues to perturb
economic and social relations in these frontier regions.

Accordingly, in an attempt to remedy this regional imbalance,
which threatened to assume alarming proportions, Belgium drew up a
whole series of legislative measures on aid to investments in the
handicapped regions. Some results have been achieved, but some
difficulties remain, and may well become more acute. Consequently,
a balanced regional policy must continue to be pursued, so as to avoid
an excessive volume of investments being concentrated in areas of
sure-fire development, by force of momentum. Thus, notwithstanding
the measures taken, inter-regional disparities still exist, which
necessitate the maintenance of an active regional policy.

Each of the countries mentioned in the foregoing section are
European countries with a unitary or central system of Government.
The brief survey is continued in this section of seven other countries,
four outside Europe, Japan, Australia, Canada and the United States
and three within Europe, the Federal Republic of Germany, Spain
and Austria. Of these, all but Japan and Spain have a Federal structure.

Federal Republic of Germany

The Federal Republic of Germany affords perhaps the clearest
illustration of the proposition that the "regional problem" cannot be
defined simply in terms of differences or disparities between regions.
Historically, the unification of Germany grew out of its separate
States and its present Federal structure, in which the individual
Länder retain a high degree of autonomy, reflects the strong sense
of regional differences and of regional community which are much less
marked in most other West European countries. The Länder are,
administratively speaking, the regions of Germany but they vary
considerably in size, in populations, economic importance and structure. In its geographical structure, the country as a whole can be
described as "unbalanced" as much as most other countries can be so

described, without, however, any implication that the imbalance constitues a "problem". Nearly one-third of the country's population is concentrated in the Land of North-Rhein Westphalia, containing the industrial Ruhrgebiet and one sixth in Bavaria, so that approximately half the total population is to be found in or close to these two Länder. A third of the population live in urban communities of 100,000 or more and there are close on thirty cities with populations of a quarter of a million or more. The concentrations of population contain the bulk, though not all, of the heavy and light industrial enterprise and equipment. The Länder vary in their economic structure - i. e. in the proportions of population engaged in primary and heavy industry, manufacturing, services and agriculture reflecting the diversity, both of the distribution of resources and their place in the complex pattern of internal and external communications.

In the post-war period, West Germany has gone through the period of reconstruction from the devastation of war to development and expansion of its economy to the degree that it has one of the highest standards of living in the whole of Europe. Its population has grown almost to that of the whole of pre-war Germany and it has attracted something like 2,000,000 foreign workers to supplement its own labour force. Though there have been fluctuations in the general economic situation, its overall unemployment rate has been of a minimal order - below an average of 1% since 1969.

Throughout this period, as in other advanced industrialized countries, it has had to face problems created by the new technologies, techniques and materials, the substitution of other sources of energy for coal, the development of road transport, the restructuring of steel and the growth of "modern" industries, in electronics, motor vehicles, chemical and modern engineering and consumer industries and services generally. Many of these changes have taken place in and affected the well established industrial centres such as the Ruhr, without creating the type of regional problem which exists, for example, in the industrialized peripheral areas of the United Kingdom, a point which perhaps emphasizes the contrasting locations of these areas in relation to the economies of the countries they serve.

All this has been accomplished under the impetus of a general growth policy founded largely on private enterprise rather than central Government economic planning. Nonetheless, there has also been a "regional component" in national economic policy derived from the constitutional requirements that the Federal Government should provide for equal conditions in all parts of the Republic. The Federal Government can exercise considerable powers, through public finance and investment and development of the national infrastructure and in other ways to ensure that general development is "balanced" with

23

due regard to the interests of the various Länder. In so doing, it supplements the self-help efforts of the individual Länder and influences and, to some extent, corrects the disparities which could arise from the fact that the Länder are unequal in resources. Inherent, therefore, in the Federal structure of Germany is a "regional problem" of ensuring a proper balance of development between its parts which would not necessarily be achieved if each Land had to rely only on its own efforts and resources.

The "regional problem" of Germany could therefore be defined as that of securing a proper balance in the development of the Länder in the common interest of the Republic as a whole. In fact, though this problem does exist and is taken account of in national policies, the term "regional policy" is more usually applied to a different and more restricted problem. Despite the general growth of the economy and the high level of incomes and employment, there are certain areas which are not well placed to share in this general prosperity. These areas are described as "economically weak" areas, their weakness being reflected mainly in significantly above average unemployment or below average national income per head. Their weakness reflects a variety of factors, from the effects of structural change, deficiencies of infrastructure, distance from main centres or rural depopulation, etc.

They consist of the zone bordering on East Germany and areas within all the Länder. For purposes of action they are currently grouped into 21 development areas based on 312 centres and encompassing one third of the total population and 58% of the land area. Since they are to be found in all the Länder, the regional "imbalance" problem is to be seen as an internal "imbalance" problem in each Land/region rather than as an imbalance between regions. The contrast with countries such as the United Kingdom and Italy is worth noting, since the key regional problem in these is an inter-regional one while the internal disparities which undoubtedly exist (for example, there are considerable differences in unemployment in different parts of the generally prosperous West Midlands in the United Kingdom) are not generally the subject of regional policy. If common terminology were used the German regional problem as formally embodied in legislation would be described as "sub-regional" to distinguish it from that of inter-regional balance.

The "sub-regional" problem would nonetheless appear to be a large one, not only because the development areas as defined cover almost 60% of the country and a third of its population, but because the stated aim of current policy is to create an additional 460,000 jobs by 1975 - more than double the total number of unemployed in the country as a whole. The implication is that these areas are to be

24

economically expanded not only to absorb their own unemployed, but to attract workers into them from elsewhere.

There is a further element in regional policy in Germany, namely, that of "Raum Ordnung" or spatial planning, corresponding perhaps to "Aménagement du Territoire" in France and physical strategic planning in Britain. The growth of the large and medium sized urban concentrations, the problems of congestion and environmental pollution and the changing land use requirements for industrial, residential and amenity use call for a planned approach to the problem of population settlement and infrastructure development. The problem is one of satisfactorily matching the utilization of land to social and economic progress. National, inter-regional and sub-regional relationships are involved. * Thus, in Germany, as in other countries surveyed, the "regional problem" is not a single one but is composed of a number of elements which add up to a large and complex task.

Since this introductory survey is intended not for detailed description but only to illustrate the nature of regional problems with which the report is concerned, the examples of Japan and Spain can be given to bring out some different aspects of regional problems from those in the previously discussed countries. The two countries are, of course, very different in many respects.

Japan

Natural configuration - islands, mountains and coastal belts - and climatic variations and the importance of overseas trade have virtually enforced a high degree of concentration of population and industry in the Pacific coastal belt. This concentration has been accentuated in the period of post-war recovery, reconstruction and industrial expansion so that by the mid-sixties nearly three fifths of the population and two thirds to three quarters of industrial production were located in this area. Correspondingly, there has been a decline in population of the rural and peripheral areas. The continued rapid growth of the Japanese economy (11.1% per annum between 1958-1968) meant also that most of it took place in the Pacific Belt. Neither unemployment nor income disparities have presented the acute social problems to be found in countries such as Italy. High growth rates have tended to reduce the income gap between the rural and the urban household, though incomes in agriculture remain lower than in industry. Population movements associated with rapid industrial growth have

* See "Raumordnungsbericht 1972 der Bundesregierung", Bonn, 1972.

25

in fact tended to diminish regional income disparities. Nor have structural changes associated with the decline of certain main industries and the need for conversion from older to new industries constituted a serious regional problem. The main such declining industry has been coal (in which employment fell from 350,000 in 1950 to 80,000 by 1971) but the effects of decline have to some extent been offset by rapid growth in industry generally.

The "regional problem" of modern Japan is not described by the traditional terms of long established disparities and decline which apply to some older developed countries. Rather, it has to be seen as an emergent one of comparatively recent origin. It is connected with the very limited land space which is available in the coastal belt to accommodate population and industrial growth and to meet rising aspirations of the people for better living and environmental conditions. The Working Party concluded (after their visit to Japan in 1970) that it had two major facets: "the external disutilities of concentration in the form of air and water pollution, overcrowding, housing shortages, spiralling land prices, water supply and transportation difficulties, etc., aggravated by insufficient investment in social capital and, on the other hand, the drainage of younger more active people from rural areas, with consequential effects on agricultural productivity, economic stagnation and difficulties in maintaining public services and facilities for the residual population at an adequate level. "*

The problem also concerns the future of Japan, for high economic growth rates and further population expansion are to be expected and, unless remedies are found, can only exacerbate the intensity of the problems resulting from these tendencies.

The changing situation which results from post-war expansion has led to an evolution of regional policy itself. Rapid industrialization meant in effect an exploitation of the advantages of the Pacific Belt. As this has filled in, become heavily urbanized, congested and environmentally inadequate the need becomes more apparent to foster growth in the other regions. In contrast with, say, Italy or the United Kingdom, it is growth rather than backwardness or decline that has created the problem areas of the developed Pacific Belt. The "regional problem" is that of finding ways to promote development elsewhere, so that the national economy continues to grow with a better balance between the most developed areas and those other regions which still have a capacity for development. Since the early sixties, therefore, it has become increasingly necessary to formulate national development policies in regional terms.

---

* "Salient Features of Regional Development Policy in Japan", OECD, Paris, 1971.

The growing affluence of the population, its demands for a better environment and the continued growth of the economy, may well demand a regional solution involving not only a proportionately higher rate of expansion outside the "problem areas" but even a contraction of the land space devoted to industry within them. Regional restructuring could thus entail an actual shift of existing industry from the Pacific Belt to other regions.

Spain

Spain has always been a country of marked regional diversity and disparities in economic and social conditions reflecting its geographical configuration, varying climatic conditions and an uneven distribution of natural resources. Economic activity and growth have tended to be concentrated in certain widely separated areas, in the central belts of Northern and North-Eastern Spain, in the Madrid area and, in the South, in and around Seville and Valencia. The size of the country and a sparse communications network has contributed to a pattern of population distribution in which small numbers of densely populated land and large urban areas contrast with vast but thinly populated rural areas, often of low agricultural productivity. The imbalance between town and country is not only demographic but also economic, with lower incomes and fewer employment opportunities in the rural areas, especially as agricultural productivity increases. This disparity produces a constant pressure towards migration from the poorer rural areas to the cities, in itself a factor which tends to reduce income disparities while increasing the imbalance of population distribution. This in itself creates new problems of accomodating an adequate infrastructure and level of services in areas suffering from declining populations.

The regional problem or problems of Spain cannot be considered in isolation from that of the economy as a whole. The key national problem has been that of securing a considerably higher level of economic activity, not only to keep pace with population growth but to raise the general level of economic welfare. Its rate of population growth, 1.06% per annum between 1960-1970, is among the highest in Europe but its GNP per head is among the lowest ($960 in 1970 compared with $2,920 in France). Efforts to promote general economic development have clearly had some success since, in the five years 1965-70, Spain achieved the highest growth rate in GNP in West Europe, and the third Development Plan predicted an average growth rate of 7% for 1972-1975. Whatever rate is actually achieved, the maintenance of a high momentum has its implications for regional development. In particular, not all the areas or regions are equally capable of rapid

27

economic expansion, so that general growth can, in the absence of special counteracting measures, be expected to produce disparate regional growth.

Because of the overriding importance of national economic growth, the regional problem has not been seen as one of maintaining the pre-existing population distribution or of counteracting migratory movements from areas of lower to those of higher economic opportunity. The dynamism of the economy involves both the creation and development of new industries in locations suitable for them and the shift from low income productivity industries, such as agriculture, to higher productivity industries, manufacturing and services, including the major growth industry of tourism. Migration and shifts in population are, in such circumstances, an inescapable concomitant of general growth. They reduce some imbalances, lessening for example income disparities as people move from low income opportunity areas to areas with better opportunities. They also accentuate others, in particular the disparity of economic conditions and opportunities between larger and smaller urban settlements and the country in between. They also create new problems of infrastructure, services and environmental protection both in the rapidly expanding centres and in smaller towns and in rural areas which are remote from the expanding areas and, not participating in the general growth, cannot command the resources needed to maintain an adequate level of services for the remaining populations.

The "regional problem" is therefore essentially not one of rectifying static imbalances but of coping with the effects of rapid economic expansion which are constantly changing the regional structure of the country. It means not only guiding regional development so that it assists the process of economic growth but also mitigating some of the effects of growth on the areas and regions which are affected in different ways. Since general growth requires capital investment, in industrial development, in infrastructure, housing and social services, the way in which that investment is promoted will shape the future regional structure of the country. The general regional problem is to harmonize the process of development with the maintenance of satisfactory balance between and within the regions. It calls therefore for a regional strategy for growth extending to the country as a whole and a combination of economic and physical and social policies to that end. Spain thus provides a further illustration of the fact that the regional problem as it is actually seen by the responsible authorities is that of the structure of the country as a whole, rather than one of individual areas.

Austria

No single formula would provide an adequate description of
Austria in regional terms.   Physically, three fifths of the country
consists of the Alpine massif; climatically there are four distinctive
zones, with varying temperatures and rainfall influencing the
distribution of agriculture and forestry; mineral resources are
unevenly distributed, with a high concentration of iron ore and coal in
Styria; demographically, over half (53%) of the population of 7.4
million (1971) live in urban agglomerations with over one quarter of
the total in Vienna and over half (56%) in Southern and Western Austria;
politically, the country is a Federation of nine Länder each, through
the large degree of autonomy in many aspects of policy making,
constituting an administrative "region".   In terms of contribution to
the domestic product, four Länder (Vienna, Lower Austria, Styria and
Upper Austria) accounted (1970) for three quarters of the total, with
Vienna at 31% approximately twice the proportion of any other Land.
Its geographical location in relation to neighbouring countries and its
differing trade relations with Germany, Italy and Switzerland on the
one hand (as well as with other Western countries) and the countries
on its Eastern borders on the other, tilts the centre of gravity of the
economy towards its Western regions.

The dynamic influences at work since the war have been numerous,
with diverse effects on different parts of the country.   The initial
period of recovery and reconstruction was followed by high general
growth, measured by GNP, sustained in the sixties at an average level
of close on 5%.   Despite an overall increase in population of some
400,000 and an influx of foreign workers, there was a net decline in
the labour force of nearly 3% so that the expansion of output reflected
an increase in productivity and changes in economic structure, decline
in agriculture, forestry and mining being more than offset by expansion
in secondary and tertiary industry and in tourism, with the emphasis
in the first half of the decade on consumer goods and in the second half
on capital goods, chemical products and "service" industries.   These
structural changes were in part in response to the international demand
for Austrian products and growth of foreign trade, particularly with the
EFTA countries.

These structural changes in the Austrian economy brought with
them certain shifts in the location of industry and employment, an
East-West shift towards the Western Länder of Salzburg, Tyrol and
Vorarlberg, a shift towards the cities and along the main traffic axes
and a tendency to rural exodus and commuting to the main cities for
work.   In addition, some 'pull' of labour was exercised in Western
areas by even more favourable economic development in neighbouring
countries, particularly Germany.

The growth of the Austrian economy has both required and occasioned the development of the physical infrastructure, particularly, energy and communications, and improvement of major North/South, as well as lateral, motorways and the expansion of motor transport. As elsewhere, industrial expansion, with rising living standards and the growth of urban concentrations, have brought with them problems of environment, pollution and congestion and the problem of conservation and protection of the countryside. The further growth that must be expected and planned for in the future will accentuate these problems.

Within this general framework of growth, development and change, the 'regional' problem of Austria emerges, not in simple contrasts between the regions (Länder) but in a variegated pattern of special problems affecting particular localities. Growth has tended to concentrate in those localities, particularly urban areas, which are well placed in relation to neighbouring countries, as in the West, or to the internal market, as in the larger centres of the East. Certain areas, within the Länder, are relatively less well placed to participate in national growth or, because of their location, economic structure may face stagnation or decline. Three particular types of area cause special concern in this respect; the border areas or regions in the East, which are both remote from the main concentrations of population and have limited access to trade with neighbouring countries; the more remote mountain and rural areas; and certain weak industrial areas, as in upper Styria, falling into decline through exhaustion of mineral resources such as coal or obsolescence of the industrial structure.

Such areas lack employment possibilities, leading to relatively lower incomes and some exodus of population. Vienna itself is not without problems, given its distance from the more dynamic areas of the West, an absence of an economic hinterland in the neighbouring countries and the stationary but ageing population resulting from these factors and all leading to a relative decline in its share of national output. Problem areas also exist in the mountain regions of Western Austria.

Regional policy can be said to have started in the late fifties when attention first began to be given to areas lagging behind general economic development. It is now envisaged as an integral part of national development policy in which a comprehensive approach to economic, physical and social development pays regard to the specific characteristics of the Länder and their varying needs.

Canada

Disparities in economic growth rates, in income, employment opportunities, unemployment and social conditions have been as marked between the provinces and regions of Canada as in most other countries. They reflect the process by which long term secular growth has distributed itself in different time scales as the country has been opened up and its resources have come under development. Canada can be described as both an advanced industrial country and also as a developing country.

In recent decades its overall expansion has been phenomenal. Between 1950 and 1972, population rose by 60%, GNP increased over five times and GNP per head over three times. The growth was uneven, population expanding most rapidly in British Columbia and Ontario while declining in proportion in Quebec, the Prairie provinces and to a larger extent still in the Atlantic region. Levels of income per head have always been significantly below the national average in the Atlantic regions and Quebec. In both these regions also labour force participation rates (activity rates) have been below the national average, while unemployment has been significantly higher. Despite its high rate of development, unemployment has been comparatively high in the country as a whole, averaging 4.2% in the 1950s, 5.1% in the 60s and 6.3% in 1972, being markedly less (about three quarters of the national average) in Ontario and the Praries than elsewhere. However, disparities in unemployment rates have not been constant. Relatively, the rate in the Atlantic region actually improved between the 1950s and 1972, falling from 176% to 143% of the national average while in the Prairies it rose from 61% to 71%.

The existence of such regional disparities, though stemming from the dynamics of development in a country of unequal regional potential, has long been regarded as a "problem" with serious economic, social and political implications. As far back as the 1930s, it became apparent that not all regions were equally well placed to share in the growth and prosperity of the country so that measures of fiscal equalization were adopted to help to augment the revenues of the weaker province to provide common standards of public services. These did not remove the basic causes of the disparities, the effects of which were accentuated in the depressed years of 1957-1961. In consequence, a number of special programmes were adopted which concentrated on particular problems of individual areas. Though these had some beneficial effects and were thought on balance to have "probably prevented inter-regional disparities from widening", it was also considered that there was "little indication that these have contributed to a stronger basis for self-sustaining growth in the lagging regions of the country". *

This conclusion led to the setting up of a special Department (Department of Regional Economic Expansion) and the policy aims for which it was established in a sense defines the regional problem as it is seen in Canada. The policy seeks to "assist in the dispersion and stimulation of economic growth - and the conditions to sustain it - across Canada so as to bring employment and earnings opportunities as close as possible to those in the rest of the country, without generating an unacceptable reduction in the rate of national growth. The policy is national in scope but it is flexible enough so that the composition of special development efforts can vary from one region to another, depending on the needs and potentialities of each one. "**

The present approach to regional development is both a multi-disciplinary and a "multi-dimensional" one - i. e. , an approach that calls for the identification and pursuit of major developmental opportunities by means of a coordinated application of public policies and programs, both federal and provincial, in cooperation, where appropriate, with elements of the private sector. This approach consists of three elements: i) encouragement of the formulation and implementation of federal and provincial policies which will provide general support for the development of slow-growth regions; ii) identification of obstacles to economic development in slow-growth regions and provision of the necessary programs to reduce or remove these obstacles; and iii) identification of specific opportunities for development in slow-growth regions and assistance in the realization of these opportunities. The framework for implementing this strategy is established by a "General Development Agreement" (GDA), and its "Subsidiary Agreements", between the Federal Government and each province.

The lessons drawn from previous experience were also that major structural changes would be required in the economy and society of low income areas and that the desired changes could be brought about only by special efforts over a long period - perhaps 10 to 15 years.

Some measure of the scale of the problem of disparities with which the policy is concerned is given by the fact that the designated "slow growth" regions to which investment incentives may be applied contain nearly 40% of the national population and labour force.

* Economic Council of Canada. "The Challenge of Growth and Change". (Fifth Annual Review, 1968).

** "Regional Development and Regional Policy: Some Issues and Recent Canadian Experience", p.59, Department of Regional Economic Expansion, unpublished mimiograph.

Australia

Australia is a Federation of six States with great variations in
climate and resources resulting in very different rates of growth and
development. The greater part of the population is concentrated in
the South-Eastern corner and in large towns and cities - 14% in the
two largest cities, Sydney and Melbourne, and a further 21% in cities
of more than 100,000 inhabitants. Despite century long efforts by
Australian Governments to encourage settlement in rural areas and
decentralization of industry, economic conditions have encouraged the
growth of the cities, to the extent that in the five years to 1971 three
quarters of Australia's population growth was located in the metropolitan centres..

The problem of "regional imbalance" is seen not so much as that
of differences in economic conditions - incomes, employment
opportunities or unemployment - between the different parts of
Australia, though these exist, as that of growing concentration in
cities. The growth of cities is in part an indication of comparative
advantages over rural and thinly populated areas, advantages in
employment opportunities and social services and amenities. In part,
however, it brings certain disadvantages, notably in urban sprawl,
congestion, commuting and environmental disabilities. It also produces
its counterpart in the rural areas, comparative lack of diversity of
employment and a weak economic basis for the support of the population
and its social needs.

The key regional problem is therefore whether a "better balance"
can be struck in population settlement by reducing the relative
concentration in large cities and fostering the growth of alternative
urban centres which can exercise a positive effect on the surrounding
country. Since Australia, as other countries, is also concerned
with economic growth, the question of how far decentralization can be
pursued without detriment to economic growth is part of the problem
of finding a suitable regional policy to cope with the future population
growth.

Population growth in Australia underlies the problem of regional
distribution. Its present population of 13 million reflects an average
annual growth rate, with large scale immigration, of 2.04% between
1960-1970 and it is estimated that it could grow by another 9 million
(70%) by the end of the century. The regional problem is therefore
one of location of population in ways which will both satisfy the
requirements of economic development and also meet social needs
for a satisfactory and viable environment.

United States

Regional problems in the United States and attitudes towards
them have to be seen in the context of a dynamic 200 million population
economy with the highest per capita income amongst OECD countries
operating in a vast and richly endowed land area that stretches from
the Atlantic to the Pacific Ocean. Economic development has been
accompanied by a continuing westward shift of population, such that
in one generation the centre of population has moved from Baltimore
to Chicago, a rural to urban movement, and a shift in employment
from agriculture to manufacturing and services. By 1972, only 4% of
total employment was in agriculture compared with some 11% at the
end of the second world war. Economic growth and structural change
has left in its wake scattered areas throughout the country where, for
one reason or another, the economic base has declined or disappeared.
Notable examples include the coal mining regions of the Appalachian
belt, the mid-Western coalfields in southern Illinois, the textiles
cities of New England and lumbering communities, farm trading towns
and many industrial towns.

On a wider definition to include rural poverty, problem areas,
as measured in terms of low income or high unemployment, are
basically those which have remained outside the mainstream of economic development and are to be found also in the prosperous fast-
growing west, the Great Lakes, parts of the mid-west, the south-east
and in the deep south. Nearly all the population growth is taking place
on the fringes of the 230 metropolitan areas which range from towns
of 60,000 inhabitants to the megalopolis of New York with its 15 million
population. Concentration of population in a very small amount of
land coupled with the declining population in city centres is giving rise
to financial and physical planning difficulties on a massive scale for
the provision of adequate public services. Rising unemployment in
the cities is recognized as a potential major problem.

Official predictions to the end of the present decade suggest that
there will be a preponderance of employment growth in the south,
south-west and north-west and that the rate of increase in the labour
force in the most populous areas will be greater than the rate of
growth of job opportunities in these areas. The underlying policy
assumption is that most of the required adjustment in matching
population and job opportunities will be achieved by internal migration
and by the natural growth of the private sector of the economy. The
concern of the Federal Government has not therefore been with that
of correcting regional imbalances as such as with that of coping with
the residual problems affecting the less fortunate areas.

The United States has had a chequered history of regional planning, largely because the notion of regionalism as a way of developing broad areas within the nation and cutting across State or local Government boundaries, runs counter to the American tradition. Originally based on assistance to a very large number of depressed communities, policy under the Public Works and Development Act of 1965 moved to one of a national integrated long-term approach based more on eco-·nomic development than on social welfare. There has subsequently been a reversal in policy as a result of President Nixon's proposals for major restructuring of Federal programmes involving the removal of the Federal presence from the Regional Commissions, except for the Appalachian Regional Commission, the elimination of the Economic Development Administration and distributing the funds previously used by them, along with some others, to the States to be used for development. United States regional policy has thus become less overtly specific and through the revenue-sharing mechanism, Federal Government responsibilities are being shifted to the State Governments.

GENERAL OBSERVATIONS

The foregoing very summary account of the nature of regional problems in a number of countries highlights those features of each country which appear to the Working Party to constitute the problems with which regional policies are concerned. Such an account does not necessarily provide a description of the way regional problems are actually defined in individual countries, either for the purposes of formulating regional policies or for presenting and explaining policies to the public.

Though in most countries, regional problems are well document-ed, in only a few countries are comprehensive descriptions or analyses to be found of regional problems in their entirety. The more frequent practice is to provide documentation about individual problems rather than the totality. This has a number of disadvantages. The nature of "the regional problem" has to be inferred from a multiplicity of descriptive and policy documents dealing with individual issues. This means that the general perspective in which individual problems are placed tends to be lacking and the particular problems treated as if they were isolated from each other when, in fact, they are not. Secondly, it conveys the impression that regional problems are "fringe" problems, outside the main stream of major economic problems such as the growth of the economy and that, consequently, they call for relatively minor measures to "correct" certain consequences, in particular "disparities" and "imbalances" which result from the main tendencies and policies which govern a country's development.

In the Working Party's view, this conception of the regional problem does not correctly represent the actual situation in the majority, if not all, the countries that have been studied. Certainly, in their origins, regional problems tended to be seen as those of localized areas with weak economic structures. It would now seem, however, to be generally recognized that this is only part of a much wider problem, namely, that of inter-regional and intra-regional "balance" in the development of a country as a whole. The commonly used definition of the main aim of regional policy to ensure a "proper" regional balance - though itself question begging until the meaning of "proper" is defined, certainly does not describe a fringe or marginal problem. It implies that some regional balance, other than would be brought about as a result of the normal working of economic and social forces and existing general policies, is desirable, and that special policies should be directed towards achieving this desirable balance.

As has been seen, regional problems comprehend a number of elements which we would summarize as:

1) The regional implications of national development policies which affect regions differently according to their potentialities and needs.

2) The regional distribution of population compatibly with various national objectives such as economic viability and acceptable economic, social and environmental conditions in the country as a whole.

3) The "balance" of economic and social conditions requisite for equitable treatment of the populations of the diverse regions.

Though the emphasis given to these problems varies from country to country, the survey suggests they are to be found in all of them to a lesser or greater degree. What is also striking is the magnitude of the problems which come within this framework. In those countries which are concerned with the particular problem of "less favoured" regions, the regions concerned may contain a very large proportion, sometimes more than half, of the total population with economic conditions substantially worse than in more favoured regions, Italy affording perhaps the most notable example. The problem of decentralization and planned population settlement can also not be considered a minor one, given the strength of centripetal forces.

The "regional problem" is thus a combination of problems, economic, spatial and land use, social and environmental, all of which call for attention and none of which can be dealt with to the exclusion of the others. Since progress in one direction is dependent on progress in the others, to lay undue emphasis on any one element would be to oversimplify the nature of the regional problem. Individual countries give different weight to economic or social and environmental problems as they affect regions. In recent years, regional policies have been increasingly concerned, not only with economic disparities but also with such problems as urban settlement, the overcoming of overcrowding and congestion of large cities, the decay of large city centres, the improvement of social conditions in disadvantaged regions or in regions of expansion, including housing, education and environment and "quality" of life as well as the protection of the environment against industrial pollution, and the conservation of amenity areas. These objectives need to be fully integrated into those of regional policies as a whole which are thus neither exclusively economic nor exclusively social.

When all the elements of the regional problem are taken together, it becomes evident that it is the problem of shaping the future regional structure of a country as a whole. It is forward rather than backward looking, and involves multiple rather than single objectives. Since a country is composed of its regions its development and growth and its social progress are the resultant of many forces which bear differently on the regions. For this reason the Working Party considers that the regional problem is best seen as an integral part of the problem of national development as a whole, including, not only economic, but also its social and environmental aspects. It is also a problem, not only for any one section, but for the community as a whole, and it is necessary to have regard to the varied wishes or preferences of people. These are normally expressed in terms of personal wishes in relation to problems of individuals or groups. They have, however, to be translated in political terms through the regional policies applicable to the community as a whole.

This concept underlies the Working Party's approach to the examination of regional policies with which the remainder of this report is concerned.

III

REGIONAL BALANCE AS AN OBJECTIVE
OF POLICY

The notion that regional policies are concerned with securing a "proper" or "better" regional balance in a country as a whole and with a wide range of general national objectives has, as has been noted, gained ground over earlier, more narrowly based concepts. The regional problem, as defined in such terms, is clearly not a small one. It implies a comprehensive approach to the management of a nation's total resources to achieve the objective, while also achieving other important national objectives, such as promoting economic growth, matching the distribution of people and employment, maintaining external competitiveness, controlling inflation, securing an efficient infrastructure and satisfactory social and environmental conditions for the population at large.

One objective of regional policy is to mobilize resources to alter the regional structure of a country. The resources of a country are not, however, infinite in relation to the claims upon them, nor do Governments have unlimited power to steer the economy of their countries in any direction they may choose. They are confined, in their actions, by basic realities, the resources available, the condition of the industries, the skills and capacities and ingenuities of the people and their attitudes or preferences towards alternative solutions to problems. Policy decisions require fine political judgements and the pursuit of certain ideal aims has to be tempered by political and economic realities.

To define the objective of regional policy as ensuring a "proper" or "better" regional balance indicates the direction in which improvement should be made. How far such an objective is attainable depends on the precise meaning that is given to the terms "proper" or "better" and the realities of life which govern the ability to carry out the specific policies or measures which would be necessary.

In most of the countries which have been studied by the Working Party it appears to be accepted that a more desirable regional balance than the one that exists or will result from the continuing processes of change is desirable. Though this does not imply that there is an ultimately desirable balance in a static sense it means that the aims of regional policy are both continuing and long term in conception. Only over a long period - so it tends to be argued - can regional policies be expected to bear their beneficial results.

The validity of this theory cannot be tested in the absence of a definition of what constitutes the desired benificial results. Unfortunately very few, if any countries, appear to find it possible to define the objectives of regional policy in any but the vaguest terms. It is difficult to escape the conclusion that the lack of clarity in defining objectives in more concrete terms partly explains both the apparent persistence of regional imbalances, signifying sometimes an apparent failure of measures in force over decades, and the inability of Governments to devise new policies which offer a greater hope of success than has attended past efforts. This situation is likely to continue unless and until the vague concept of "better balance" is clothed with more precise definitions which take account of the real situations with which Governments are actually faced.

The need for more precision in definitions of objectives is of course greater the wider their range and the greater the degree of priority given to them over other important objectives. No country is so wealthy that it can afford to pursue policies without regard to their effectiveness in securing the desired results, or policies which involve attaining one set of aims at the expense of others which may be equally desirable. The OECD countries are pledged to pursue policies aiming at enhancing their economic capability, with due regard to social needs and the qualitative aspects of life, including environmental needs. Regional policies must therefore be tested against the same criteria as apply to other important objectives and this entails an effort to clarify and render more precise the practical implications of the concept of regional balance. In this chapter the concept is further examined in order to bring out some of its more important implications.

One notion can be discarded at the outset. "Proper" regional balance cannot, and in practice does not mean a precise equality of economic and social conditions throughout a country. All the countries that have been studied are "imbalanced" in one way or another, and the imbalances reflect the fact that nature has not evenly endowed every part of a country with the same capacity to support human life. Climates and soil, ecological and physical configuration differ, and affect the uses to which land can be put for agriculture, industry and commerce. Natural resources, minerals, water supplies are unevenly distributed. The location of ports and harbours, navigable rivers, mountains, hills and plains affect the location and direction of principal communications and the siting of towns and urban conglomerations in relation to each other. The industries and occupations which can flourish depend not only on the physical presence of the materials and resources they require but also on the influence of international trade, which by the operation of the principle of comparative costs, determines the international division of labour and the degree of specialization in each country. In countries which depend on international trade both the location and growth of industries are very much conditioned by the working of international competition.

It is not surprising therefore that each country that has been studied is markedly unbalanced. Population tends to be heavily concentrated in certain areas where conditions are, or have been, most favourable for the industries and occupations in which the country specializes or has specialized. The economic structure of each region also has a different proportion of different industries reflecting the relative suitability of the underlying conditions for particular activities. The size of towns, the degree of urbanism, densities and the balance of population distribution between town and country also reflect the working of the same forces which influence a country's economic structure.

A pictorial representation of geographical imbalances would show, for virtually every country, a different relationship or balance between each part of the country, according to the feature depicted. In terms of area a country can be divided into equal parts thus:

Figure 1

    8 regions of
    equal area

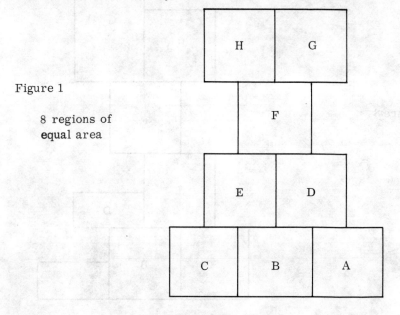

41

In terms of (working) population the same regions would show a different proportionate balance, thus:

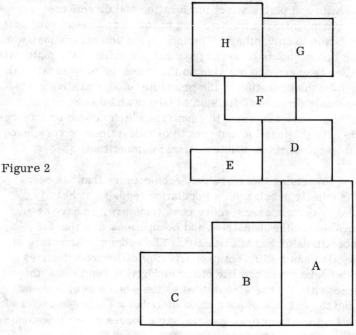

Figure 2

In terms of employment in agriculture they might show:

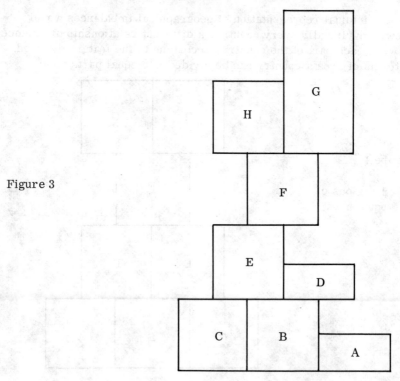

Figure 3

42

In terms of employment in manufacturing industry they might show:

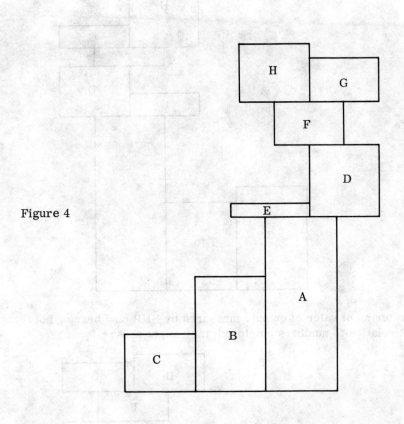

Figure 4

In terms of employment in certain "other" industries (such as "service" industries) they might show:

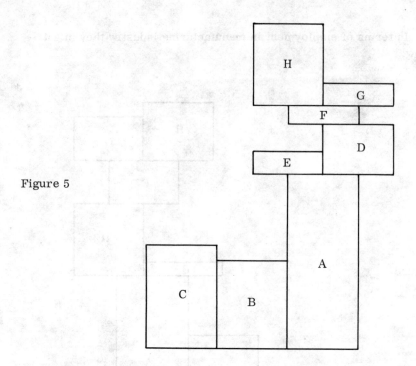

Figure 5

In terms of value of output, measured by GNP (and bearing no direct relation to numbers employed) they might show:

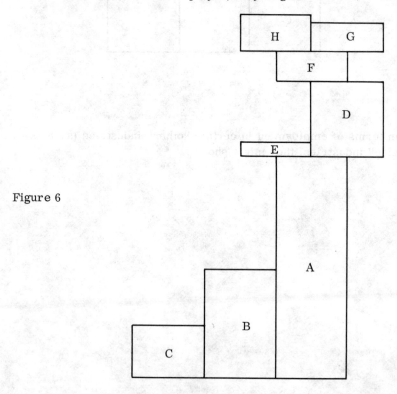

Figure 6

Inevitably, if there is imbalance in one direction there must be a corresponding imbalance in all. A similar variety of shapes would be found in presenting the distribution of occupations or skills by regions, or of populations in urban concentrations of given size.

A variety of shapes would also be found in the distribution of wealth and incomes, corresponding to capability of different industries to produce incomes for those who work in them.*

The disparities which result from the uneven distribution of a country's resources and economic occupations are of course not static. The constant changes in the fortunes of individual industries, as old equipment and methods are superseded by new, as techniques and technologies change and as new competition emerges in other regions or as new resources are discovered and developed produce a kaleidoscopic series of changes in the regional structure of a country. The more dynamic a country, the greater its population growth, the more rapid its acquisition of new skills or better education, the higher its investment in productive equipment or economic and social infrastructure the more noticeable are likely to be the differences in the 'shapes' of the regional imbalances between two periods. It is safe to say that few countries have shown an unchanging regional pattern over a lengthy period of time.

Changes in the regional pattern are therefore to some extent a mark of the dynamism of the economy, and lack of change may also signify a static or stagnant quality. The differences between "old" and "young" countries might well be indicated by the degree of change in regional shapes.

Adaptability to change takes a number of forms, each of which will affect the regional pattern. The decline of old industries and the introduction of new produces shifts in industrial location. Increased affluence changes consumer tastes and preferences, and produces an effective demand for more varied and higher quality products, for amenities, recreation and tourism. Improvements in education and skills increase both the supply and the demand for industries which can utilize them. Since each industry has its own locational requirements - e.g. tourism tends to be elsewhere than old industrial areas - response and adaptation to these changes imply a changing regional pattern.

* NOTES:
    (1) A table giving the arbitrary but self consistent values on which the figures are based is as follows (see Table page 46).
    (2) This technique has been used, e.g. in Sweden, to present various features of the regional structure in graphic form (see pages 47 and 48).

TABLE OF PROPORTIONS

REGIONS	WORKING POPULATION	AGRICULTURE EMPLOYEES	MANUFACTURING INDUSTRY EMPLOYEES	"OTHER" EMPLOYEES	GNP
A	10	0.5	6.0	3.0	40
B	7	1.0	4.0	1.5	20
C	5	1.0	2.0	1.8	10
D	4	0.5	2.5	0.8	12
E	2	1.0	0.5	0.4	2
F	3	1.0	1.5	0.3	5
G	4	2.0	1.5	0.4	5
H	5	1.0	2.0	1.8	6
Country	40	8.0	20.0	10.0	100

46

Fig. 1:1. Two pictures of Sweden

A. The proportional area
of the counties*

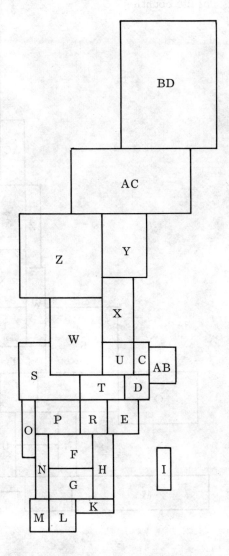

* The letters stand for the individual counties, as follows:

AB	Stockholm	K	Blekinge	T	Orebro
C	Uppsala	L	Kristianstad	U	Västmanland
D	Södermanland	M	Malmöhus	W	Kopparberg
E	Ostergötland	N	Halland	X	Gävleborg
F	Jönköping	O	Göteborg and Bohus	Y	Västernorrland
G	Kronoberg	P	Alvsborg	Z	Jämtland
H	Kalmar	R	Skaraborg	AC	Västerbotten
I	Gotland	S	Värmland	BD	Norrbotten

47

B. The proportional population
   of the counties

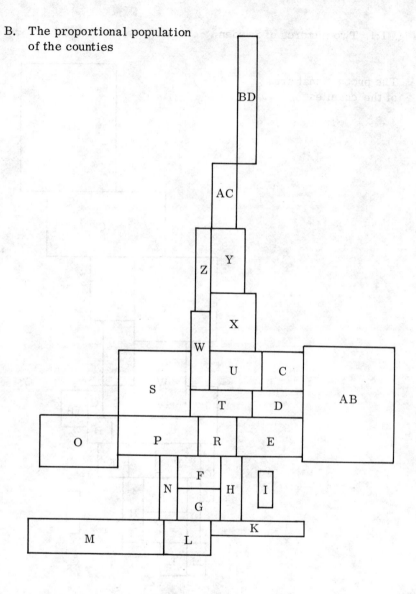

The urge for self-improvement and for higher earnings produces
a shift between occupations, as people opt for those occupations which
give them a better reward for their talents and energies.   Insofar
as the areas in which they are born and grow up cannot provide such
occupations they face the choice between accepting a lower standard
by remaining where they are, or moving to where they can find better
opportunities.   This can mean migration to other parts of the country

or even abroad. In some cases, of course, the alternative to migration is commuting over long distances to work, e. g. in frontier areas. In no country that has been studied have internal and external migration ceased to be an important element to the process of change.

Normal and "Abnormal" Disparities

It should be clear from this analysis that regional change and regional disparities are an inherent feature of all societies and that the mere recognition that there are differences between regions of a country can afford no guide to what may be meant by establishing a "better" or "proper" regional balance. Nor do expressions such as "equality" of incomes or employment opportunities offer much help without allowing for the inequalities between people in their capability to earn incomes or utilize the given employment opportunities.

In most of the countries studied the difficulty of giving objective content to such expressions tends to lead to the view that what constitutes a "better" regional balance must in the last resort be a matter of subjective and highly political judgement. This is evidently true, but it has the disadvantage of subjecting Governments to pressures for regional policies which may bear no relation either to what is desirable for the country as a whole or feasible, having regard to the actual economic problems or to the resources that can be utilized for the purpose of securing a better balance. The difficulty may be accentuated where self-interested regional pressures on central Government can be brought to bear through regional institutions and pressure groups. The overall national interest can be in conflict with the apparent interest of particular regions or local areas, but the pressure of special groups and interests may often be more effective than the resistance based on a less well defined national interest.

In a number of countries attempts have been made to overcome this difficulty by establishing certain criteria, embodied in legislation, for identifying areas and regions to which special measures, usually for granting various forms of assistance to local authorities and industry, can be applied. The technique that is used is basically simple. It involves using certain statistical indicators such as incomes per head and unemployment and discovering how far they fall below the national average. Areas for assistance can then be defined as those that fall below the average by a given amount. The system has the merit of limiting the total number of areas qualifying for assistance according to policy decisions, and enabling assistance to be con- centrated on those areas deemed to be most in need of assistance.

It cannot however be pursued too far. In view of the uneven distribution of people and industries and the dynamic influences at work in every economy there will always be imbalances which can be shown statistically without any implication that they should be eliminated to bring about an artificial evenness throughout a country as a whole.

It can, of course, be the case that national output can best be expanded, or national growth achieved, by applying more resources to the utilization of the capabilities of regions which fall below the national average performance. Whether this is so or not must depend on the circumstances of the region. It is not theoretically impossible that, properly developed, a hitherto below average region can be turned, by national effort, into a region of above average performance. In so doing the national average will itself change and some other regions may fall below it. This is but a theoretical possibility. In practice the difficulties of bringing severely disadvantaged regions, such as the Mezzogiorno of Italy, up to the national average, are manifest.

The Working Party does not ignore or reject the argument that "social" reasons can justify the diversion of resources to give assistance to less favoured regions and that it can be economically, socially and politically beneficial to promote a better balance in economic life and social conditions as between regions. What is at issue is how to give suitable expression to this aim in a world in which regional disparities are a "normal" consequence of the whole process of economic development.

There are other reasons why the use of simple averages to measure disparities affords an inadequate guide to policy. Statistics are by their nature only rough and ready indicators of the real situation. In comparing differences in average monetary incomes and earnings account has to be taken of the real values. Low monetary incomes can in some cases be associated with correspondingly low costs of living or better environment. Moreover, areas of low average money incomes may nonetheless be areas in which, for the same class of worker, earnings are as high as they may be in other areas, the difference in average being due to the proportions in which different income groups are to be found.

Similar observations are relevant to the use of other frequently used indicators of disparities such as employment, unemployment and "participation" or "activity" rates (the proportion of the available work force (people of working age) in employment). Average regional unemployment rates may not only conceal considerable differences between areas within regions. Unemployment percentages among, say, coalminers may be equally high in regions in which average

unemployment rates over industry in general are very different. Low
activity rates may reflect the age and sex composition of the population
and differing skills and the economic structure of a region which is
unsuited to their employment. Low average income may also
characterize regions particularly suited to retirement, without
signifying that the active population have lower incomes than people
in similar occupations elsewhere.

Not until the reality behind crude statistics is investigated can a
useful distinction be drawn between "normal" and "abnormal"
imbalances.

Another approach to the problem of defining the "better balance"
which regional policy seeks to achieve is to accept that there are
"normal" imbalances and disparities - in other words that differences
in averages are not in themselves a problem - but that "abnormal"
or "excessive" disparities are. This is, of course, also question
begging but it does help to get closer to the problem. Differences in
incomes or the variety of employment opportunities available in
different regions are usually tolerated in most societies when they
reflect differences in skills and aptitudes for different types of work.
What is less tolerable, firstly to the people concerned, and then to the
social conscience of society, is a situation in which income earning
opportunities are well below people's talents and skills, where people
are persistently unemployed or under-employed for long periods and
where large numbers of people are obliged to accept poverty, squalor
of living conditions and a detrimental environment without hope of
betterment.

This is only partly a regional problem. In some countries the
severely "underprivileged" part of the population is largely concentrated in certain regions, the most notable example being that of Southern
Italy. In the majority of countries, however, it may be found in all
regions, mostly in the larger concentrations of population, particularly
in large cities. The important thing from the point of view of regional
policy is that its regional distribution does not fit simply into the
pattern of high and low average income regions. In the United Kingdom,
for example, while average incomes are somewhat lower in Scotland
and the North than in London or the Midlands, the problem of poverty
and social distress is a characteristic feature in the outworn inner
cores of the large cities in prosperous and less prosperous regions
alike. The same is true of the United States, Canada, Japan and many
of the other countries. It is not exclusively confined to the cities,
since in areas of rural and industrial decline emigration may leave
behind those ill equipped to maintain a satisfactory existence. Measures
to deal with such problems may have to be of a general social character
but the way in which they are distributed regionally cannot be left out of
account in devising policies to secure a better regional balance.

51

What is needed, therefore, before regional policies aimed at a better overall balance between regions can be formulated in meaningful terms is an evaluation of the importance of the various - often numerous - indicators, not only separately but in combination with each other, each indicator being weighted according to its relative importance. Comparisons between regions would be made on the basis of all the relevant indicators taken together rather than singly. There are, of course, no precise and objective criteria to determine what weight should be given to different factors, e. g. the condition of housing and amenities versus the level of employment or incomes. Political or subjective judgment would be involved. But even a subjectively weighted combination, rather than a series of indicators, each treated separately as a basis for action, would enable greater precision to be given to the definition of objectives of regional policies. Progress in this direction is already being made in some countries.

Population Settlement

As has been noted the problem of regional balance is not only an economic one but also that of population distribution, the size of cities and the relation of town and country. The problem of defining the desirable balance is not less difficult.

To accommodate population growth satisfactorily quite clearly requires a more ordered use of the total land space. It is a regional problem par excellence, for it concerns the relative growth of different regions and the organisation of growth within regions. The various policies which seek to achieve a better balance of population distribution - Raumordnung in Germany, Aménagement du Territoire in France, land use strategic planning in the United Kingdom, decentralization in Austria - and planned settlement and development policies in many other countries are as much part of the problem of regional imbalance as the disparities in economic and social conditions.

Here again, however, to state the problem in terms of an "ultimate" objective of "better balance" does little to define the more practical problem of what actually constitutes a satisfactory and yet attainable balance. Most countries now recognize that this problem is not one that can be isolated from that of economic balance or of economic development. The need to ensure both employment and an adequate living standard in accordance with the resources and skills of the population means that the geographical distribution of population must be related to the distribution of economic potential. Economic policy, land use and physical planning strategies are therefore two aspects of the same problem of securing the best practicable regional balance of all the activities of a country in the general interest of all its inhabitants.

Economic welfare considerations influence population settlement policy in a number of ways. Towns and settlements require an economic base, i. e. the ability to provide work and income earning opportunities for the people. They cannot therefore be placed, or made to develop to a predetermined size unless they can satisfy the requirements of the industries for which they may be suited. Industries will not move voluntarily to new and expanding towns if their needs cannot be met more satisfactorily than in their existing locations. Any substantial change in the pattern of settlement is therefore only likely to be feasible if it improves the conditions for operation of industry and commerce. Restraints on the growth of existing cities, to secure a better balance between cities or between town and country, will carry economic cost to the country if the alternative locations are less advantageous. All settlement, especially of urban populations, requires expenditure, mostly in the public sector, on the necessary infrastructure, of communications, water and power, etc. The amount of reshaping of the pattern of settlement that is possible will therefore depend on the availability of resources for this purpose and the relative urgencies of need in both older and newer centres of growth.

As with economic imbalances, statistical criteria provide an uncertain guide to the criteria for securing a better balance. Variations in population densities, in ratios of socio-economic classes, of manufacturing and service industries, of health and education services or of cultural facilities are inherent in the diversity of the conditions which govern the structure of urban settlements. Comparisons with theoretical optima, or averages, region by region, or town by town, cannot establish the possibilities of development in given areas, or the consequences for other areas of restraints in overgrown or congested zones.

Almost all countries, even those that are mostly densely populated can find more than one solution to the problem of balanced settlement. The choice may be between encouraging or permitting the expansion of those cities or centres which still have a capability of growth, of creating a number of new growth points, or of seeking a wider dispersion of growth centres as opposed to a more concentrated pattern. In many countries too the number of potential new growth points may exceed what is required, after allowing for the capability for expansion of existing cities.

Subjective and political judgements, as well as local pressures are likely to play as great, if not a greater part in the final decisions on what should be the better regional balance to be aimed at. Unless such judgements and pressures are brought within the economic capability of a country the objective of a better regional balance might be achieved only at the cost of a weakening of its economy. The studies made by the Working Party suggest that few countries have as yet reached the point of formulating strategies for regional development on a basis which takes sufficient account of its economic implications. Until further progress can be made in this direction, judgement can only be reserved on whether countries will succeed in their attempts to secure a better regional balance in their population settlement.

Differential Growth

The concept of securing a better regional balance, whether in economic life or in population distribution implies a policy of differential rates of growth of different regions and localities within them. The general idea is that the present balance is unsatisfactory and that by appropriate regionally-differentiated measures, a more satisfactory balance can be achieved at some future, usually unspecified, date, often a long way ahead, in some cases the end of the present century or beyond. This concept needs examination, for on its validity depends not only the success of the regional policies which are being increasingly pursued but also the prospects of successfully coping with the problem of enhanced economic and social development. Regionally differentiated policies provide an alternative, or modify, those global and nationwide policies which are designed to strengthen or raise the condition of life of the people. A central issue for the management of the economy of a country is how far regionally differentiated policies will be compatible, or in conflict with the more general objectives.

It may be said at the outset that regional differentiation is not necessarily in conflict with general growth. Countries have always, and inevitably, developed at a different pace in their various regions, reflecting their diversity of resources and opportunities. Some regions have progressed more rapidly than others and some have declined as their resources are exhausted or as population migrates to regions of greater opportunity. The pattern of rise and fall, absolute and relative, has never been static at any time of history in any country and it must be regarded as totally unrealistic to imagine that future change will not be regionally uneven.

If all factors were perfectly mobile the problem would be a simple one. People and capital would move from regions of lower to regions of higher opportunity until an equilibrium was reached at which further marginal movement would cease. All people - category for category - would be equally well off in their respective regions and though these would show disparities in average incomes or standards of life no one would gain by moving to another region. The marginal return on capital would also be the same in all regions, so that further movement of capital would cease.

Such a theoretical situation is remote from reality (a) because there are obstacles and costs to free movement of people and capital, (b) because it brings with it unacceptable social disadvantages, (c) people are not governed only by the economic calculus and (d) market forces do not act smoothly and rapidly enough to permit easy adjustment to changing conditions. Neither people in general nor entrepreneurs in particular have full knowledge of alternative opportunities in unfamiliar areas or regions and their attachment to their own part of the country lessens readiness to move or to transfer enterprise.

In practice interregional adjustment is at best only partial. Some movement of both people and enterprise takes place under the pressures of need, some migration occuring to regions of higher opportunities and some movement of capital and enterprise to regions where human and material resources are underused or unemployed.

The well known contrast between "workers to the work" or "work to the workers" depicts the basic alternatives which arise from the normal process of change and in practice no country that has been studied either seems or has been able to depend solely on one or other of these modes of adjustment.

It is, however, this choice at the margin which lies at the root of the problem of regionally differential policies. The point that deserves emphasis is that the way this choice is exercised has important general economic implications, for the development of the country as a whole and for its separate regions. By and large the choice is not exercised in a uniform way throughout the OECD countries.

In certain countries, such as the United Kingdom and Italy, the emphasis of policy is on "work to the workers", excessive net outward migration from backward or declining regions being regarded as at best a socially undesirable consequence of the difficulty of moving sufficient work to the workers. In the United States and in Spain movement of workers to where job opportunities arise or can be created is regarded as a feature of the dynamic growth of the whole economy. In countries in which the regional balance problem is not so much that of disparities as of securing a well distributed growth, regional policy envisages the movement of both people and jobs to those locations which are considered to be favourably placed for development. Growth centres, new towns, maritime and industrial areas, counter magnets and off-setting capitals are all instances of a method of regional differentiation of growth which is not based exclusively on one or the other extremes.

Policies of regionally differentiated growth can only achieve their objectives if sufficient resources are applied to them. Regional policies with the comprehensive purposes which have been described are policies involving the use of a nation's resources to achieve one pattern of regional development rather than another. The larger and the more ambitious the aims the greater must be the diversion of resources away from general development to the areas and regions selected for more rapid growth - whether to "catch up" with other regions or to develop more rapidly because they are deemed to be favourably placed for development. Whether this process leads to a greater or less rate of national development must depend on how well the policy of regional differentiation coincides with that of overall growth.

There are several reasons why it is desirable to study the economic implications more closely. Firstly, failure to assess the scale of regional differentiation needed to achieve the desired regional balance may mean that insufficient resources are applied, and the solution of the "imbalance" problem is not merely deferred but is put off indefinitely. Secondly, the diversion of sufficient resources to achieve one aim may diminish those available for other aims of equal or greater importance. Thirdly, if the policies of regional differential growth are on a scale that call for resources which are not available, it becomes unrealistic to pursue them and necessary to consider the alternative options for regional development.

These observations are prompted by the facts of experience in a number of countries. The designation of large parts of countries and large proportions of area and population as "problem areas" - in Canada, United Kingdom, Italy, Germany, Scandinavia, Belgium, Holland, etc. , means that the regional problem is a large scale one in such countries. The persistence over decades of "unacceptable" regional imbalances which have not so far yielded to vigorous regional policies, e. g. Italy and the United Kingdom, suggests either that insufficient resources are available or that the methods employed are not well enough attuned to the nature of the problem.

The fact that regions of high growth and "prosperity" have themselves become "problem areas" of an opposite kind, through over-concentration and congestion, requiring policies of deconcentration and dispersal, both increases the resources required to deal with these problems and to alleviate them by alternative development else-where in selected areas. The question can well be asked whether, since few countries have sufficient resources to meet the needs and aspirations of their peoples in all parts, regional differentiation policies are feasible in any meaningful sense. The dilemma that many Governments face is that problems requiring the use of resources exist in all parts of a country, and, if all that is possible is to give a marginal degree of preference to some areas over others, the possibility of securing a preconceived desirable regional balance must be very limited.

The problem can be illustrated in abstract and theoretical terms. The "average" economic growth of a country (however measured) can be shown over time as a line on a logarithmic chart, an even rate of growth as a straight line, thus:

Fig. 6

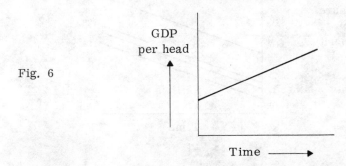

Differential regional growth can be shown by similar lines converging or diverging with the average and with different points of departure representing their uneven levels, thus:

Fig. 7

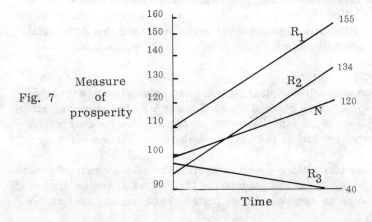

57

Figure 7 shows the evolution of a measure of prosperity, such as Gross Domestic Product per head, over time in a country (N) and in three of its constituent regions. R_1, starting at a higher level of prosperity than the country as a whole, and R_2, starting at a lower level, have both progressed more rapidly than the country. Some other regions must therefore have progressed less rapidly than the national average. One such is R_3. The disparities between R_3 on the one hand and R_1 and R_2 on the other have widened, while in the particular illustration given those between R_1 and R_2 have remained constant relatively and widened absolutely.

If all regions were to progress at an equal rate the picture would be:

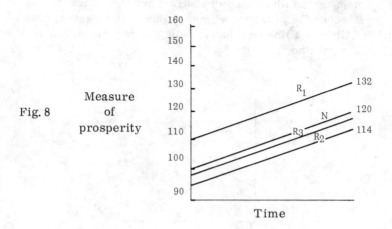

Fig. 8

Measure of prosperity

Time

In this case all regions have doubled their "level" and while they have remained in the same relative position the "absolute" gap between them has also doubled.

All that this shows is that equal rates of growth, whether high or low, will not alter the relative position of regions to each other but the absolute difference between them will widen; and that differential rates of growth will alter both the relative and absolute differences between regions.

A region with a lower starting point can only catch up with other regions at some future point of time, if it has a higher relative rate of growth. The lower its starting point, or the smaller its differential rate of growth, the longer the period needed before it can catch up.

There are two factors which determine the relative rate of growth between regions. First the potential of the individual region for growth by utilization of its own resources, material and human, second the degree to which there is a net transfer of resources from one region to another, raising the rate of growth in the receiving region and diminishing it in the exporting region. "Resources" can be in manpower or capital. This is a complex issue. If, as a result of intervention by means of regional policy, regions with previously unused resources receive a higher share of a nation's investment, whether the latter remains initially unchanged or is simultaneously increased, the ultimate outcome is likely to be an increase in national output, while productive potential and output in the non-assisted regions might or might not have been reduced. There is not necessarily a net transfer of resources from the non-assisted to the assisted regions.

The ability of a country to transfer sufficient resources between regions to bring about a given differential rate of growth must clearly turn on the magnitudes involved. To secure a more rapid rate of growth in 1% of a country than in the remaining 99% is a small problem for the 99%, given that there is something to develop in the 1%. Conversely it is a large problem if it is the other way round, virtually infinitely large, unless there is an extraordinary degree of concentration of the nation's wealth in its 1% region.

A policy of regional differential growth based on transfer of resources has of course an effect on both, on the region to which they are transferred and on the region from which they are transferred. The effect on overall national development turns on the gain in growth of the receiving region, on whether it is greater or less than the diminution, if any, of growth in the exporting region. It is clear that overall national growth must suffer if resources are transferred on a large scale from where they can secure a high return - in economic and social benefit - to where they can obtain a lower one. In making this comparison between rates of return, however, the appropriate costs to take into account are the opportunity costs, which, in the case of immobile unused resources - a part of the unemployed or under - unemployed labour force in the assisted regions, for example - are likely to be below the nominal cost to the individual entrepreneur.

This is of course the nub of the problem that faces the policy makers on the allocation of resources between regions. The problem must be regarded as an important and acute one in most of the countries which are now pursuing regional policies for it is evident from the facts given in Chapter II that regional policies are concerned with very large scale problems. The areas and populations which form the object of regional policy measures range up to a half of the total land space and population. Both "disadvantaged" and selected growth regions are capable of absorbing a large proportion of the marginal resources available for development from national growth.

Some of the former are those in which natural conditions for development tend to be relatively unfavourable. Were that not so they would not be as much in need of special attention as other regions. On the other hand there are regions which are in need of assistance because their former basic sources of employment have been contracting so rapidly that even otherwise normally favourable conditions for development might not be sufficient to redress the situation. Such rapid loss of former basic employment may occur in agriculture, mining or manufacturing and may be due to technical progress, exhaustion of mineral resources or change in demand conditions - all this without necessarily signifying that the regions affected are unsatisfactory locations for new forms of economic activity. Regions which are not "disadvantaged" but have been selected for some special development effort presumably offer special advantages.

It needs to be said that it is not the case that high national growth rates necessarily enable policies of regional differentiation to be more easily and successfully pursued. The opposite may be true in some cases, for high national growth rates may simply reflect the opportunities that exist in more favoured regions. In Italy, for example, high national growth rates reflect the rapid post war advance of the North accentuating the problem of enabling the South to keep up with national growth let alone catching up with that of the North. The Swedish experience has been that high general growth makes for a large net migration and a low growth diminishes this migration. In the comparatively slow growth economy of the United Kingdom (due, in part to its already higher state of development and moderate growth of its population and labour force) such net growth in employment as has taken place has been largely outside the areas designated "development areas". High growth can accentuate regional disparities simply because some regions are better able to expand their economies than those which lack either industrial resources or skills. High national growth can, of course, generate additional resources for use in the less favoured regions but it also "feeds on itself" and does not guarantee the possibility of higher rates in the regions with the most obstacles to development. By the same token the concentration of resources on the development of the less favoured regions may lessen rather than augment national growth. It can work either way.

There are differing views about the extent to which policies aimed at achieving a better balance in regional development can, on the one hand, be pursued without paying a price in terms of moderated national growth rates, and, on the other, achieve higher national growth rates through bringing into use immobile and otherwise under-used resources, avoiding congestion costs in other regions, etc. Insofar as a price has to be paid, it is clearly a matter for political judgment what price is worth paying. If there is some sort of trade-off between national growth and socially and politically desirable inter-regional balance, then clearly the democratic process and the machinery of government must decide the point at which the trade-off should be struck.

It would follow that, in formulating policies for regionally differentiated development, it would be advantageous to assess the magnitudes involved, the scale of the problem and the impact the policies and the resources applied to them are likely to have, on both national growth and its future regional balance. It must be acknowledged, however, that only the roughest prognostications can be made about many of the facets in question and sometimes policies will have to proceed by a gradual feeling of the way rather than by a hard and fast determination of objectives to be achieved by means which, quantitatively, have equally been subject to a hard and fast determination. Despite the difficulties, however, attempts to quantify all aspects should be persisted in.

The studies of the Working Party have shown that very few countries have attempted, so far, to calculate what is really implied by their regional aims in terms of resource utilization and the effect their policies are likely to have on the actual regional balance of the country. So long as this is so the danger will exist either of not allocating sufficient resources or of diverting resources to one part of a country on a scale which may increase the difficulties of dealing with problems elsewhere. In both cases there may still be failure to achieve the desired satisfactory balance over the country as a whole.

The conclusions which emerge from this discussion of regional balance as an objective of policy are two fold. First, it can be misleading to base the definitions and criteria for establishing the aims of regional policy - the meaning of "better regional balance" itself - on simple statistical comparisons such as deviations from the national average of incomes or unemployment or employment, migration or proportions engaged in high or low income occupations. Secondly, the more we are able to make overall evaluations of the magnitudes involved in the "imbalance" problem and of the real prospects of achieving differential rates of growth from given policies and resources, the better, provided we do not delude ourselves by adopting spurious estimates.

IV

THE NATIONAL SETTING FOR REGIONAL POLICIES
AND THE INFLUENCE OF CHANGE

Whatever aims may be sought by regional policies, action takes place in a world of constant and rapid change. The economic and social fabric of society is moulded by a host of influences. Some are only short lasting in their effects, others permanently altering the "parameters" of problems and possible solutions alike. Some changes occur which, for a time, may be but dimly perceived, creating a time-lage before policies are adjusted to a situation which is "new" only in the sense that it is newly and belatedly noticed.

The complexity of the modern world, the rapidity with which important changes occur and the difficulty of gauging their existence or effects makes it futile to suggest that regional policies can be easily and scientifically and frequently adjusted to changing circumstances. Policies that are continuously and rigidly pursued can, however, only lead in the wrong directions and ultimately to frustration and failure. It is not surprising, and indeed is necessary and right, that most countries recognize the need for "flexibility" in their approach. The fact, however, that regional policies have evolved increasingly towards more comprehensive aims, denoted by the concept of a better regional balance over a country as a whole, makes it all the more necessary that flexibility should be based on awareness of the way the broad influences which affect the country's development also bear on its regional problems.

Such awareness is necessary too if the right judgements are to be made of the effectiveness or otherwise of the policies that have been pursued in the past, and of the need to change them in relation to the future. All too often, such judgements overlook the influence on regional balance of factors other than regional policies themselves and, therefore, wrongly commend or condemn the policies. New policies are then proposed or devised, based on a mistaken appraisal of past experience and misconceptions of what they may be able to achieve in the future.

The national influences which bring about regional change can be classified, broadly, as demographic, economic, technological and social, each subdividing into a multitude of different aspects. It is no part of our purpose to describe them in detail or to attempt to depict the way they have influenced regional problems in each country. Our aim is only to draw attention to the manner in which they bear on "regional balance" and, therefore, are relevant to the shaping of regional policies. The point should be made, however, - and it is one which is germane to all discussions of regional problems - that they are all interrelated inter-se. The regional balance in any country, in other words, is the outcome of all these influences, acting in combination.

Demographic Influences

The population of a country changes according to the balance of births and deaths and the net external migration, and these will reflect age and sex composition, fertility, health, social attitudes to birth control and family planning, and economic opportunity. In none of these matters is there any necessary correlation between change in national totals and those in individual regions unless, of course, they were to have a very high degree of homogeneity. Changes in the total size or composition of the national population may, therefore, be accompanied by quite different changes in the size and socio-economic characteristics of the populations of the individual regions themselves. Indeed, even when the total national population is stable in terms of international migration and/or natural change, a significant redistribution of population may still occur by reason of inter-regional migration and/or differential natural change rates at the regional level.

This in itself cannot be considered to be either an economic or social problem unless there are insufficient means to support the population at standards which are deemed acceptable. The importance of demographic change is that it is one of the originating causes of change in regional balance and poses the question of how the regional organisation of a country, its economic life and its physical structure should be adapted, not only to the total number of people to be accommodated, but to its changing composition.

Clearly, policies of equal growth of each area or centre of population would make no sense and would indeed create new imbalances between people, their economic opportunities and their environment, for neither natural increase nor age and sex composition change in equal proportions throughout a country. Demographic change, therefore, necessitates a continuous and variegated adjustment in the pattern of location of people, even were there to be no significant change in the nature of economic activity or in economic and social conditions generally. It is not taking sides on the issue of whether some migration is either desirable or acceptable to assert that demographic change is itself a cause of unequal development and must be allowed for in formulating local and regional policies. What allowance should be made for it, and the degree to which it may be necessary to foster or check migration movement must depend on the importance of the other major national influences at work.

Economic Influences

Generally speaking, regional policies, as they have evolved in the majority of countries, tend to be focussed on the differences between regions particularly in the state of their economy and their capacity to satisfy the needs and aspirations of the people. These differences are usually seen as arising from the unequal distribution of resources due to differences in regional structures - the dependence of some regions on industries of low income or employment generating capacity, while in others, the industrial structure is more favourable in these respects. Regional economic policy seeks, in such circum-stances, to bring influences to bear which will improve the economic structure of the weaker, poorer, or disadvantaged regions, both absolutely and relatively to those of other "more favoured" regions. In this way, so the argument goes, a more equitable distribution of the country's economic activity may be secured. It may also serve, and it is sometimes an explicit aim or hope, to enhance the economic "performance" of the country as a whole, by better utilization of the resources of the "disadvantaged" regions which are under-used or not developed as well as they might be.

This approach tends to obscure the fact that there are other economic influences at work, besides those of regional economic policy and those which are internal to the regions concerned. There are those economic forces and policies which have a pervasive influence throughout the economy as a whole, and hence on all the regions. They affect not only the general level of a country's economy, manifested by changes in GNP, average income per head, employment and unemployment, etc., but also the regional economic balance of the country. Unless account is taken of the way they do so, regional policies cannot be geared to the real situation. In most countries

65

studied, regional policies and the resources used to back them up are, despite the ambitious nature and even major importance of their aims, still a relatively minor influence compared with national economic forces and policies.

An influence or force which might well deserve to be placed at the head of any list is a country's need for, and vulnerability to, international trade. Economic growth of most advanced countries and the majority of OECD countries is closely related to the development of international trade. Most countries are, in varying degrees, heavily dependent on imports not only of raw materials for their industries but also for many of the consumer and capital goods which they either do not produce themselves or in which other countries have a comparative cost advantage. Whatever methods of economic management it uses to achieve an equilibrium on its external accounts, there will be effects on those industries which are important to its internal trade and, therefore, in the regions in which those industries are located.

When it becomes necessary to encourage exports or diminish imports, it becomes inescapable that there should be a relatively greater expansion in those regions which can produce the exports or the import substitutes. It would, in most cases, be purely fortuitous if they happened to coincide with the "disadvantaged" regions of traditional regional policy.

It is sometimes argued that disequilibria in external trade are essentially a short-term phenomena, so that in the long-term, there need be no incompatibility between the objectives of regional policy and those necessary to maintain international competitiveness. There can, however, well be an element of wishful thinking in such arguments. It is evident from post-war economic history that, in some countries, disequilibria in external accounts have been as persistent and deep-seated as regional imbalances themselves. If, in such cases, the disadvantaged regions are not well suited to a country's international trading needs, regional policy may lead the country further away from the goal of strengthening its international trade. In that case it may face a real dilemma, between pursuing its regional policies to the detriment of its trading position and, possibly, its overall standard of economic life insofar as it depends on international trade and competitiveness, or modifying regional objectives to improve its international performance, even if this leads to a further widening of disparities in growth rates between the more and less favoured regions.

It is not appropriate to offer any opinion on where the balance of advantage lies in individual countries. What can be said, however,

is that the pattern of international trading is itself constantly changing, as previously underdeveloped countries increase their industrialization, as new market groupings are formed and as currency and
monetary policies alter the relative competitiveness of different
nations. Assessment of the likely effects of these changes on the
national economy and their bearing on its regional structure and
imbalance problem, is an essential prerequisite for devising regional
policies suited to a country's real needs.

The same is, of course, true in regard to all other major
influences on a country's economy. The aim of most countries is
to achieve a specified rise in real GNP over a period of time, for the
benefits it will bring in improved individual living standards, in
making more resources available for social services and the development of infrastructure and for strengthening external balance. The
necessary means include increased efficiency and productivity in
industry, modernization and re-equipment of manufacturing industry,
exploitation of new national resources, educational and vocational
training, retraining and relocation, and so on. In this process,
competition presses on those industries which do not or cannot adjust
and enables others to expand or replace them. GNP may rise or fall
with the short-term fluctuations of the economy but, in the longer
term, a sustained growth is brought about only by processes which
transform the economy as a whole.

The process of sustained rise in GNP can, therefore, often both
accentuate the difficulties of the "disadvantaged" regions and further
increase the interregional disparities. For example, the necessary
improvement in industrial efficiency and productivity may have a
considerably larger impact on the older industries whose equipment
and manpower utilization may be much more uneconomic than in the
newer industries. This applies with particular force in many
countries where agriculture is in process of raising its productivity
by increased mechanization, higher yields per hectare and development of large-scale farming. The exodus from the land is accelerated and, while GNP may benefit, the regional problem is given a further
twist, particularly if alternative employment opportunities are lacking
in the regions affected.

Similarly, the modernization, restructuring and improvement of
productivity in the traditional "heavy" industries, such as steel,
shipbuilding, etc. , by which greater output per employee in a
declining market leads to continued run-down in manpower employed.
Both the internal regional structure and the relative balance with
other regions where more modern and expanding industries can better
absorb workers made redundant by productivity improvements, are
adversely affected.

67

If migration is not practicable, either because of unwillingness to move, or the difficulties of providing accomodation in the better off regions for those who would be willing to move, the growth of GNP can well be achieved only at the expense of more unemployment in the declining regions and greater disparities between them and the others. By contrast, where policies of planned population settlement are based on the provision of expansion areas, outside as well as within the regions affected by such changes, migration may play a greater part in adjusting regional balance to the growth in GNP.

Fluctuations in the national economy are a further instance of the national influences which affect regional balance and the policies which may be feasible to deal with it. Periods of accelerated growth and expansion, sometimes inflationary, tend to be followed by at least a pause succeeded by a degree of recession until enough change has taken place to bring about a renewed period of expansion. Cycles may vary in length and depth, but almost all economic history, including that of the post-war period, has been characterized by a succession of upswings and downswings. Italy, Germany, France, the United States, the United Kingdom, Spain, Belgium, to mention only some, have seen such movements in the last decade alone.

In regional terms such fluctuations tend to have certain well observed effects which are not uniform between regions. In periods of upswing of market expansion and economic optimism, industrial capacity is more fully utilized, output and demand for labour are increased. The effects are most marked in the regions whose economic structure enables them to respond to these factors. Unemployment may fall generally, until the available supply of labour is fully absorbed in some regions, to the point often of inflationary pressures on wage levels, to strains on capacity, "bottlenecks" in production and other symptoms of "overheating". In the regions with backward or declining staple industries, this point may not be reached at all before the economy starts on the next phase of recession (brought about either by a natural "running out of steam" or by governmental measures to "apply the brake" or counteract inflationary pressures).

During the upswing, or in its later phases, unemployment in the backward or declining regions may continue to fall after the point is reached where no fall is possible in the overheated regions. The disparities in unemployment, the ratio of unemployment levels between regions may even tend to move in favour of the backward regions. Any inclination to attribute this to the beneficial effects of regional policies must be tempered by the fact that the backward or declining regions are usually precisely those which are capable of a slower and smaller response to the pressures of the upswing, and can therefore only begin to "catch up" in the later phases. Upswings tend to be of limited

68

duration and, while they may effect some improvement in the economic situation of the backward or declining regions, they do not necessarily alter basic structural weaknesses.

In the downswing the converse process will operate, but unless there have been significant structural changes in the backward and declining regions, their unemployment situation will worsen relatively since they are subject, not only to the influence of the overall contraction, but the reasons for their structural weakness will have remained, adding structural to cyclical unemployment.

It cannot be ruled out, on purely theoretical grounds, that fluctuations in the economy as a whole might bring about some long-term improvement in regional balance. For example, if the upswing is of sufficient duration, it might encourage the establishment of new industries in the less favoured regions, either because of the limited capacity to expand in the "overheated" or congested regions, or because regional policy measures have some effect.

There is, however, little concrete evidence on this point and some would point in the opposite direction. The key to changes in the basic economic structure of regions, and in regional balance, is long-term investment. Only if a country's capital investment is directed in increasing proportion to the regions which are backward or declining or those chosen for expansion, can there be any long-term improvement in their favour. In the downswing, however, investment tends to be stagnant or even decline. In the upswing it is likely to be in those industries with the best long-term growth prospects, the "modern" rather than the staple old industries.

Much of the new investment in many cases takes place through the installation of new equipment where industry already exists and by the adaptation of existing buildings, both combined with a more efficient use of capacity and labour. The amount of truly mobile industry is small in most countries, compared with the total industry which remains where it is. Since the "problem" regions are often such because of their disadvantages - in situation, lack of labour skills, poor infrastructure, and so on - it would seem optimistic indeed to expect that a short-term upswing will significantly affect the regional direction of investment in favour of the problem regions.

What is perhaps of even greater importance is the fact that, in periods of downswing, little progress can be hoped for in overcoming those structural imbalances which are such an important part of the regional problems. Periods of downswing can be as long as, or sometimes longer than, periods of upswing. In any given period, say ten years, there may be three, four or five years of downswing. The

69

implication is that, in calculating the length of time which it will take for regional policies to have effect in promoting more investment in the problem or expansion areas, it is necessary to allow for the years that are "lost" as a result of economic fluctuations. *

As regards the regional working of other important economic influences, in essence, the general point applies - that they all affect "regional balance" in many ways which do not necessarily coincide with the formal objectives of declared regional policies. They may indeed outweigh and nullify those policies, so much so as to justify the observation that the "true" regional policies of a country are denoted by the way national influences and policies work in practice rather than by those limited policies which are specifically termed "regional". It is observed, for example, that some countries had smaller regional income differentials than others when regional policies were started. Among the factors behind this was the degree of industrialization.

Among such other influences are the monetary and fiscal systems and their associated policies. These affect the level of inflation, the net transfer of resources, between socio-economic groups, the public and private sectors and regions and areas, as changes occur in the systems and weight of taxation, in the purposes and priorities of public expenditure. Change in the ratio between direct and indirect taxes, the incidence of taxation on consumer and producers, the allocation of public expenditure between defence, administration, industry and agriculture, research, infrastructure and the social services, will in total affect regions differently. They act, in fact, to change the regional balance, even when there is no specific intention to do so.

The way in which social and economic tensions are resolved may have a profound influence on regional problems. In the field of incomes and earnings, wages and salaries, the manner in which they are determined, and the bargains struck between employers and employees of major groups, may change inter-regional income disparities and levels of employment according to the regional distribution of the employees involved. Common national wage standards, when there is a shortage of labour in some regions and a surplus in

* It may be pointed out as a useful example that in the United Kingdom, fixed capital expenditure in manufacturing industry fell in real terms from 1961-1963, from 1966-1968 and from 1970-1972, i.e. in six out of twelve years. It seems unlikely that much progress could have been made in those years in changing the "persistent and deep-seated" imbalances which have for so long been the main feature of the United Kingdom's regional problem.

70

others, inhibit the working of the market forces of supply and demand whereby the price is adjusted until supply and demand balance. Progress towards social equity by equalization of income has been more marked in some countries than in others. Desirable though it may be, it may also mark progress towards the perpetuation of unemployment in the regions in which there is a larger work force than can be absorbed by existing industry, unless mitigated by the outward migration to regions in which, at the given "price" of labour, the employment opportunities are larger.

Again, no judgement is implied. The example shows only that changes in incomes and wages, and the system for determining them have an important influence on regional problems and the solutions that can be found for them. This and the few examples given should suffice to establish the general argument with which this section is concerned that it is necessary to appraise the influence of national economic forces on regional problems before effective policies can be devised.

Technological Change

Technological change has a major influence on national economies and on regional structures and balance. The development of new products, the use of new materials and of sophisticated techniques and devices in the organisation of production are not confined to any one, or to a few, activities but find an application in virtually every industry, primary, secondary and tertiary, in communications by land, sea and air, in environmental control, health, education and scientific research. The changes it brings about affect output, markets, demand for and supply of materials, manpower and skills, and the complicated network of linkages, internal and external, between producers. They create new tastes and consumer prefer- ences, affecting attitudes towards work and leisure, especially as more sophisticated techniques replace traditional processes requiring the use of the individual brain or hand. They are, increasingly, the principal means by which countries can hope to see a rise in their GNP and standards of living, accompanied by less work and more leisure, improved environment and more amenities of life and facilities for sport, recreation, tourism and other leisure pursuits.

In so doing, they "free" man from many of the more arduous tasks that can be more efficiently and economically done by the new equipment and techniques. They also increase the scope for activities which still require the individual. The observed fact that, in more advanced countries the proportion of people engaged in "service" occupations of distribution, leisure and cultural life is increasing, is associated with this underlying change in the techniques of production.

There is, however, a reverse side to this somewhat rosy picture. The blessings, such as they are, of rapid technological advance (leaving aside the controversial issue of whether they lead to over-exploitation of the world's resources at the expense of future generations), are not evenly bestowed on all countries or all regions alike, nor have they as yet eliminated poverty and backwardness. They can pose new problems, partly inherent in the experimental nature of many new developments, their high capital cost and the drastic effects that sudden introduction of new technologies can have on the fortunes of long-established traditional industries.

It is clearly impossible to generalize about the regional effects of technological change. Neither beneficial nor adverse effects are likely to be confined to particular types of regions. The new technology industries themselves vary considerably in their location requirements. Some are labour-intensive, able to make good use of unskilled labour in regions where it is abundant. The requirements of some, more capital intensive, can sometimes be met more readily in less developed regions than in more advanced regions where existing industry may be resistant to change or where pressures on available facilities, sites and communications deter new entrants. The "location requirements" of the "Service" industries in particular are different from those of primary and manufacturing industries and the shift in the balance towards service employment also has its implications for both regional development and regional population distribution.

Social Influences

Economic and social change interact, affecting and affected by each other. Economic development changes not only the means available to satisfy needs, but alters the needs themselves. It influences the socio-economic composition of society, the size of different income and occupational groups and the pressures of "effective demand" that they can exercise on the production of goods and services of all kinds. It alters the need for different skills, imposing its own demands on education and training and altering the employability of people and the length of their working life.

Social change is, however, not only a response to economic change but has a momentum of its own. It reflects changes in outlook and values, in concepts of equity and justice, of the value of health,

72

education, leisure and improved environment. The "quality of life" is not an abstraction but a social quality. The importance attached to it in the fairly recent past has undoubtedly increased, competing in public esteem and priority with internal economic aims.

All such changes have their implications for regional balance and for regional policies. They affect people's preferences for urban and rural life and for social and cultural pursuits. They, as well as economic pressures, influence people's choice of location. In societies where urban values predominate, they lead to a flow from rural areas to cities and from some urban areas to others. Not all people are desirous and able to move to the location of their choice but many, particularly the younger, are and do.

Not all parts of the country are equally endowed with the ability to meet people's social needs as they are also not equally endowed in economic matters. Nor is there any identity in the ability of any city, area or region, to meet economic and social needs alike, for some may be ideally placed for economic development but yet be ill-suited and unattractive to the people required for that development.

Regional policies aimed at securing a better regional balance have, therefore, to bring about some sort of "marriage" between economic and social structure and to take account of changing social as well as economic influences.

The complexity of the task can be illustrated by reference to education. The development of education, by raising the minimum school-leaving age and extending secondary, higher and vocational education, not only helps to provide the skills and professional qualifications required by the changing technical requirements of economic life, but also changes people's aptitudes and interests. Horizons are widened creating not only "social mobility" - movement of people between socio-economic and occupational groups - but physical mobility, as people seek out the places where they can best meet their needs and utilize their skills and talents which education has developed.

The regional problem which arises from the advancement of education is two-fold. Educational facilities have to be provided and scope found for the utilization of the talents that education stimulates. This usually means an increasing regionalization of the institutions of higher education, the spread of universities, polytechnics and centres for professional and vocational training more widely. At the same time, it changes the occupational "mix" of the population and, unless the geographical distribution of occupations corresponds, physical movement of people to where they can put their talents to use becomes necessary.

As higher education increases, the number of people suited to administration, management and the professions, and the problem of providing a proper regional balance in employment opportunities extends to these groups as well as to those engaged in manufacturing processes. This is, of course, part of the problem of securing an acceptable regional balance in services employment. Since all industries and people themselves have their own, and often different location desiderata, the problem of matching employment to people can only be resolved if sufficient attention is given to the changes in people's abilities and outlook that result from educational progress.

Implications for Regional Policies

It is not necessary to elaborate on the way these national influences affect the regional problem in each country. No two countries are alike, in their population or economic growth, in their response to technological change or in the nature of the social forces at work. Our brief survey does, however, enable certain points to be emphasized which are of more-or-less common application.

The influences and changes that have been outlined are important in them all. They cannot be ignored in attempts to secure a better regional balance, in whatever way this may be defined, because, as has been seen, they work on regional balance itself. They will operate in future and affect the regional balance of the future. Assessment of future trends in these major national influences is as essential to realism in regional policy as it is to those policies which are national in concept and seek to guide, modify, control or stimulate the general progress of the nation.

This does, of course, add a new dimension of difficulty in determining what regional policies should or could hope to achieve. The future is always obscure. The most modern techniques of forecasting are still so open to errors from insufficient data, lack of knowledge of what has actually happened in the past, and from the plain fact that surprises must always be in store - the unforeseeable cannot be foreseen - and that prediction is largely an exercise in crystal-gazing.

As has been noted by many observers, short-term or medium-term predictions can be even more difficult than for the longer-term. Action takes place in the present and it is impossible to foretell what the response of governments and people will in fact be to situations which arise at particular points in time, since usually, there is a large variety of alternative ways of dealing with immediate situations.

Longer-term predictions are only possible on the basis of assumed trends which may be closer to reality if they are made within a wide enough range, and are steadily corrected as new knowledge becomes available and is absorbed. Since changing the regional structure of a country is generally accepted to be a long-term objective, this offers some consolation but does not, of course, remove the difficulty of allowing properly for future trends.

The problem of difficulties in prediction and the need to improve data collection, methods of interpretation and forecasting is, however, a general one. It is not confined to regional issues and bears on the formulation of national and regional policies alike. It does not alter the fact which it has been the aim of this chapter to demonstrate, that national influences have an important bearing on regional problems and have to be taken into account, as far as it is practicable to do so, in forecasting policies aimed at securing a better regional balance, however this may be defined.

The Working Party attaches a good deal of weight to this conclusion. The studies it has made show that, over the years, there has been an increasing recognition that regional problems cannot be understood or treated in isolation from national problems. In many countries and in international bodies, this realization has, however, yet to have its full influence on the way regional policies are formulated and co-ordinated with those policies which seek to deal with "national" problems, economic and social alike.

Recognition that national and regional problems are part and parcel of each other and that the influences that bear on the one also bear on the other, has important implications. It means adopting an integrated as opposed to a compartmentalized approach, both to the evaluation of the problems themselves and the impact that policies can have on them. A country and its regions are still one country. The overall evolution of a country can be no more and no less than the evolution of its regions. Policies which are conceived of in terms of global national objectives will, nonetheless, be policies that will have regional effects; conversely, those policies which are regional in concept and intention will, in total, affect the country as a whole.

Failure to recognize the interrelation of national and regional problems may lead, self-evidently, to the adoption of conflicting objectives and to policies which may be mutually frustrating. Thus, a certain rate of national economic growth may be desired that is attainable only through an alteration in the country's regional economic balance. If this is, for social, political or other reasons, an undesirable one, growth and regional balance will be in conflict. Only if they are considered together can policies be adopted which will

achieve the two objectives according to the relative importance attached to both of them.

It is, of course, this very problem of deciding what weight should
be given to possibly conflicting objectives that makes it necessary
to evaluate the influence on the regional problems of the national
factors which have been discussed in this chapter. Policies are not
made feasible simply by wishing them to be so. They are only made
feasible by the decisions on the allocation and use of resources which
are required, which in turn, depend on what resources are available
and the competing claims on them.

Evaluation of the likely trend of the national influences is, therefore, essential in a number of ways. It will show how the regional
problem itself is likely to evolve in the absence of measures to change
its course. It will show what resources will be generated by economic
growth and how they will match up to the claims on them that will
arise from population change and the satisfaction of their economic
and social needs at whatever levels may be deemed to be realistic.
By itself, it can give no indication of the feasibility of attempts to
change the regional balance. For this, a complementary evaluation
is necessary of the effects of national trends on the regional structure
and of the response which regions may be able to make to them.

It is, thus, only by the evaluation of national and regional factors
in conjunction with each other, that a valid answer can be found to the
question of how to achieve a satisfactory or better regional balance
compatibly with other objectives of national policy. The fact that
different countries pursue the objective in different ways - some by
accepting the need for movement of people to where the economic
basis can be provided, others by seeking to move economic activity
to where people are or wish to remain - indicates not only differences
in social philosophy but also in the national setting of the regional
problem and the evaluation that is made of its relation to national
problems.

It must be added, however, that if the evaluation is not made at
all or is made on the basis of aims themselves rather than on an
adequate appraisal of the factors which influence national and
regional problems, it cannot be expected that regional policies
will have the results that may be desired of them.

Results have indeed not always come up to hopes or expectations,
even in countries in which regional policies have been pursued for a
long time and with substantial resources. There is more than one
reason for this but we do not hesitate to ascribe it in part to a failure
to assess all the elements that are involved in finding solutions to
regional problems, among them being the way the major national
influences bring about regional change.

V

THE NEED FOR STRATEGIES

The previous chapters have shown that, as regional policies have evolved, their scope has in fact become wider, as the objectives extend from "problem areas" to "problem regions", from single to several regions, from several regions to "regional balance" of the country as a whole, and from regional balance as a problem in itself to regional balance as part of the wider and longer-term problem of regional structure in all its aspects, economic, physical and social.

However different the pace may be in different countries, the evolution towards wider concepts and aims also leads to an evolution of the principles, methods and techniques which countries have employed as they identify those issues which call for a regional approach to national problems. These change, not only because the problems themselves change but because countries are continually learning from their own experience, and perhaps also from those of others which have been earlier in the field. This process never stops and is not likely to. It reflects not only the uncertainties about what the goals of regional policy should actually be but the truly experimental nature of the efforts that most countries have made hitherto to reach them.

It is no criticism of Governments to say that regional policies are in an experimental stage, even in those countries where they have existed longest. They are of comparatively recent origin in the world's history. Regional change has always occurred, with both desirable and undesirable effects but it is only over the last decade or so that the notion has gained ground that Governments have both the duty and the power to guide that change in the general interest, and not simply to intervene with palliative measures in particular places.

Neither academic studies of the mechanisms of regional changes, nor empirical investigation of the working of regional policies have as yet progressed far enough to produce any concensus view on what constitute the "right" or more effective methods of securing the aims of regional policies. The approach of Governments is itself - inevitably so in in a political world - pragmatic rather than theoretical. Pragmatism and "practical politics" are stronger forces in the development of policies than theory. It is when the gap between them becomes too wide that "practical politics" may lead into the practice of the impracticable.

It is axiomatic that no policy will be adopted unless it is "practical politics". It is equally axiomatic however that more than political acceptability is required to make a policy work in practice. The methods adopted must be suited to the objective, and the objectives must be attainable by the methods adopted.

The history of regional policies has amply demonstrated that the choice of objectives and methods are interdependent. As the area for which special regional measures were deemed necessary widened, from smaller districts to larger development areas and regions, so did the range of measures themselves, from direct stimuli to industrial enterprises through grants, loans and taxation reliefs to indirect encouragements through remedying deficiencies in infrastructure and environment. As the regional problem was seen to be, not only that of the internal situation in particular problem regions, but also of interregional disparities and growth rates, the range of measures extended further, seeking to modify the interregional imbalance by inducements in some and restraints in others; or by influencing national investment according to regional objectives; and, as physical planning or population distribution objectives became more explicitly an aspect of regional policies, so it also became evident that these could not be dealt with in isolation from the objectives of regional economic policies.

Whenever numerous and interconnected aims are sought simultaneously the problem of choosing the best method is both "strategic" and "tactical". The fact that regional policies have, over the years, increased in scope, and in the variety of measures by which it is sought to carry them out, has reinforced the need to consider the broad "strategic" issues which underly the choice of methods and specific methods. The remainder of this chapter is concerned with such issues, leaving the examination of specific methods to the next chapter.

Most OECD countries appear today to accept - at least in principle - the need both for a "strategic approach" to regional policy and for bringing its aims into some sort of harmony with other major aspects of national policy. There is however no uniformity in the manner in which this is done. It is done most explicitly in the countries which have adopted systems of comprehensive national planning, in which national targets are set for a given period ahead and revised at periodic intervals. France, Italy, Japan and Spain offer examples of national comprehensive plans which also include the objectives of regional policy and the way in which these relate to the other purposes of the Plan. In some others regional policies may be set out separately from other objectives of national policy, in comprehensive statements of regional economic or population settlement, policies, as, for example, in Canada, Australia, Germany and Austria. In the United Kingdom and United States reliance appears to be placed less on comprehensive indicative plans, either national or regional, than on the individual specific policies in which regional objectives are included.

Theory alone cannot prove which of the alternative systems are likely to yield the best results. Comprehensive "indicative" planning or more "ad hoc" and partial systems depend alike for their results on the validity of the data on which they are based, the realism of the objectives, the scale of the resources applied to different purposes and the effectiveness of the detailed measures which are employed. Systems which appear theoretically more satisfying will break down, or fail to achieve the desired results, if there are failings in their practical application. Conversely, practical realism, combined with adequate knowledge of the relevant facts, may offset a lack of theoretical "order".

The test by which a strategy can be judged is not, therefore, whether it conforms to one or other "system", of comprehensive or "ad hoc" policy formulation, but whether, in either case, it takes sufficient account of all the elements in the problem. The more numerous and complex these are, and the more they are interrelated and mutually affect each other, the more necessary it becomes to consider them together, before a policy can be determined - or be made effective - in any particular direction.

It is because regional policies have, in many countries, reached this stage that it becomes more necessary than in the past, to adopt a systematic approach to regional policy formulation, so that the strategy which is adopted - whether expressed in comprehensive planning documents or otherwise - reflects a balanced approach of all the elements which interact upon each other and together determine the regional evolution of a country as a whole.

The essence of a "strategy" is that it is a unifying concept, defining and clarifying the individual objectives and bringing them into a coherent whole. It shows also how the methods employed are related both to the objectives and to the criteria which govern the

choice between them. Consideration of the principal elements involved, in both objectives and in choice of methods, is therefore a first
and necessary step towards the development of an effective and fruitful
strategy for regional policies.

A strategy designed or required to influence the regional structure of a country as a whole will in practice be a combination of
strategies, with different authorities and institutions, central Government and local authorities (or, in Federal countries, the Federal
and State Governments) public institutions and organisations in the
private sector, all having a part to play. The implementation of a
general strategy is an organisational problem. This is a subject to
which attention is given later on in this report. It is mentioned here
to avoid confusing the elements of regional strategy itself with the
tasks of the institutions or organisations which may be involved in
carrying it out. The fact that there are usually many such institutions
also reinforces the need for establishing an overall strategy to provide
a common framework for the activities of all the participating or
cooperating bodies. Without this, the conflicts of interest and rivalries
between them may act to nullify or frustrate the attainment of their
separate objectives.

The fact too, that regional aims can be applied to different aspects
of national policy, e. g. economic, social, physical planning, and be
nation-wide, inter- and intra-regional and even local in scope,
enhances the need to bring the separate aims and methods into some
sort of coherent relationship with each other.

In short, a regional policy can only be judged, for its suitability
and effectiveness, by the extent to which each element in it finds its
place within a common general perspective.

The Elements of a Systematic Strategy

A broad classification of all the elements can be based on the
distinction between:

a)   The facts constituting the problem or problems.

b)   The principles governing the choice of policies and methods.

c)   The policies themselves - definition of objectives and
     selection of methods.

This also indicates the logical order in which to build a strategy.
It is not, by any means, the order which is actually adopted in practice.

The Working Party has observed that in many countries c) tends to be placed first. The disadvantage is that the solutions or policies adopted are directly geared to the objectives and may fail, or only partially succeed, if they are based on an inadequate appraisal of the facts involved in choosing between alternative objectives and methods. The disadvantage is still greater when the ultimate objectives of regional policies are themselves vaguely defined. As has been noted, general objectives, such as "correcting" or "removing" disparities, or seeking a better balance are themselves question begging. They can only be made more precise, and become an adequate guide to policy when the preliminary work on a) and b) is satisfactorily undertaken.

Each of these three broad groups can be broken down into the components or elements which need to be studied or evaluated.

Assessment of regional facts, group (a) includes the recognition and survey of those problems which are to be designated as "regional", i. e. requiring a regional approach in policy. Secondly it includes appraisal or diagnosis of the origins, causes and consequences of these problems. Unless there is such a diagnosis, solutions based on objectives alone represent only the treatment of symptoms, a practice which is no more likely to be successful in the regional policy sphere than in medicine. Thirdly it includes distinguishing between those regional situations which are "acceptable" and those which are not. As has been noted, many of the current definitions of "unacceptable" situations, such as disparities in employment, unemployment, incomes or economic structure are arbitrary in the extreme and cannot be used as pointers to policies until they are refined so as to distinguish between those disparities which are a "normal" feature of a dynamic society and those which are so "abnormal" as to require special measures to eliminate them or reduce their effect. It is difficult to see how any policies or strategies can be realistic, or their objectives feasible, unless each of these three tasks has been adequately carried out.

It follows from the evidence in previous chapters that part of the task under (a) includes an examination not only of the internal situation in individual regions, their structure, comparative strengths and weaknesses, advantages or deficiencies, and the internal influences at work which may change them, but also an assessment of the influence that the "national" forces at work - those described in Chapter IV, will have on the regions, individually and in relation to each other.

It is believed that a systematic appraisal, on these lines, of the factual background would show that the "regional problem" cannot be adequately defined in the somewhat one-sided way that has been traditional in many countries. Emphasis on one particular aspect, or on the problems of particular regions, obscures the interrelation between regions and the fact that each region will have problems - often the counterpart of those in other regions - which require measures of regional policy to deal with them. If, for example, a list were drawn up of significant indicators of regional disparities it would be found that "backward" or "less prosperous" regions might not compare unfavourably in all respects with those classified as more advanced, prosperous, etc. Thus the problems of congestion, over-crowding, housing shortage, environmental pollution and the associated high costs of transport and rents or levels of local taxation needed to overcome these deficiencies may be characteristic of the major urban centres in the "prosperous" regions. They are part of a country's "regional problem" and have to be allowed for in the overall regional strategy in which proper weight is given to all the problems in the national situation which have a specifically regional distribution.

It is reasonable to suggest therefore that Governments that seek to develop effective strategies should give adequate - and in most cases this means increased - attention to their techniques for evaluating the facts with which regional policies are supposed to deal. One improvement which the Working Party's studies suggest is particularly needed is the establishment of a comprehensive range of indices which, taken together, and each given its due weight, will adequately describe the true nature of the regional problems, and the degree of differentiation that needs to be made between regions in working out policies that will have regional as well as nationwide objectives.

The establishment of such indices would also be a first step towards providing a better basis than exists at present for international comparisons, the need for which can be expected to grow as regional policies themselves become a matter for international concern.

Principles governing the choice of policies and methods, group (b). This general heading can also be broken down into separate parts. It includes establishing the range of policies and measures which, in individual countries will come into consideration; the criteria for selection of policies and measures from that range; the factors which limit the choice and, finally, appraisal of the possible impact of selected policies and measures.

The traditional "problem orientated" approach to regional policy has the disadvantage of obscuring the fact that the same "regional problem" can be dealt with in a variety of ways, by methods of quite different character. That this is so is evident from the different ways in which countries which appear to have similar problems, actually tackle them.

The policies that can affect regional problems include those directed towards industry, investment for growth, modernization and efficiency, "conversion" or substitution, and towards influencing its location; land utilization and physical planning policies to facilitate development in accordance with concepts of town and country planning, growth centres, nodal points and the like; infrastructure policies, to provide the social equipment, roads, communications and institutions needed for economic and social life; social policies, in education, health and welfare; public finance policies by which the resources required from public funds can be applied to different competing aims; administration policies by which organisation can be adjusted to the tasks to be accomplished; and those national policies which, without having a specific regional purpose, nonetheless bear, directly or indirectly, on the regions.

Each of these policies not only influence the way the regional problems evolve but also present alternatives to each other. In countries, such as the United States where economic development tends to be regarded as the domain primarily of private enterprise, the public sector policies for regional development are largely in the field of infrastructure. In "mixed" economies industrial policies may be regarded as equally suitable for State intervention as those in the "public sector" itself. In Federal States some of the policies will come within the sphere of the Federal Government and others within that of the component States.

There clearly can be no a priori rules for determining which of these types of policies will be the most effective in given circumstances. Each of them will almost certainly be relevant to some degree. Judgement has to be exercised and, in the last resort, it will be political judgement that will be decisive. This will reflect political pressures and social philosophies as much as any purely technical assessment of the merits of the alternative policies. If the judgement is exercised, however, with insufficient regard to their merits it should not occasion surprise if the results do not come up to expectations or desires.

Assessing the merits, or the advantages and disadvantages of policies within the range of those that are possible involves more than one consideration. Each of the broad policies can be applied in more than one way, and in each case questions of principle will arise which favour one way rather than another.

Thus policies directed towards improving the industrial structure of a region or regions pose a number of questions. For example, in a "declining" region should the effort be directed towards the older, existing industries, to remove the causes of their obsolescence or, alternatively, should their run-down and eventual disappearance be accepted and new industries be established in their place? If so, what kind of new industries? The choice can be a wide one, between manufacturing or service industries of different kinds, ranging from distribution, office employment to tourism. The determining factors will not be only the ability of the region itself to meet the requirements of the industries concerned, but also the way in which external conditions affect those industries. Thus a region may be well suited for the expansion of a certain manufacturing industry but if it is not better suited than other regions or if the industry itself faces a contracting market or greater foreign competition the room for overall expansion may not exist. In such a case expansion in one region may be possible only at the expense of contraction elsewhere, which may or may not be desirable, and it may be preferable to expand other industries which do not entail such consequences.

The appropriate regional industrial policy may also vary according to the importance attached to international competitiveness, the need in a given region for labour rather than capital intensive industry, the stimulation of small rather than large scale enterprise, the avoidance of inefficiency and low productivity and perpetual subsidies and the desirability of locally owned or controlled industry rather than externally based. It may turn too on what needs to be done, in the way of infrastructure, to adapt a region to the kind of industrial growth contemplated, and the costs of so doing.

Similar considerations arise in other fields. Land utilization and physical planning policies pose numerous choices. The number and size of growth centres, nodal points, urban concentrations will depend on the general physical planning strategy, the ability to encourage the movement of both people and employment opportunities to the selected growth areas; dispersal or concentration, the balance between urban and rural areas will turn on assessment of such factors as communication, access to markets and supplies and the timing and phasing, and costs of providing the necessary infrastructure in relation to the projected rate of development not only of individual towns and centres but also of all of them taken together.

Public finance policies may be utilized to give preference in the allocation of resources, to particular purposes, social as well as economic, and to regions. How much preference is feasible depends on the relative urgency of needs and the budgetary and fiscal policies required for control of inflation, maintenance of the value of the currency and the policies which determine the contributions of central and local Government respectively. The principles which are applied to public investment, e. g. the degree to which a minimum return may be required from all investment, irrespective of purpose, and the way in which return is measured, also influence the extent to which public finance policies can be applied to regional purposes.

Similarly, national policies can in principle be modified to suit regional purposes, but how far this is practicable will depend on the importance attached to national rather than regional purposes. The "national interest" may require the maintenance of industries for national security - defence and food production, advanced technology, etc. - or a high degree of competitiveness as a condition of national economic viability. Such requirements may not be compatible with a regional strategy which diverts or concentrates resources in excessive degree to regions which lack what may be required for these national aims. On the other hand it may be possible to utilize regional policy in ways which enhance the attainment of national ends. Part of the problem of devising a regional strategy is therefore that of reconciling national and regional objectives.

Finally, the choice of regional strategy must also be governed by the fact that different policies, within the range outlined, can be expected to have a different impact on the regional problem or problems with which regional policy as such is concerned. Assessment of this impact is essential to determine which regional strategy is likely to be more feasible and necessary than others, within the limits which are set by the resources available to the country as a whole and the principles by which their use is governed.

In the last resort policies must deal with the real situations that will exist, after allowing for all the efforts that are made to change them. Only if the impact of alternative policies is correctly estimated can a choice be made between strategies, policies or measures alike which will deal most effectively with those real situations. The point may be illustrated from the experience of those countries which have, so far, failed to achieve the regional "balance" which they deem desirable. Insofar as they have failed, the alternatives are to reinforce the measures that discriminate in favour of certain regions, or to accept that the desired balance is not in fact fully attainable. Whatever conclusion is drawn the strategies and policies will need to be modified accordingly. For example, failure to provide sufficient jobs in Southern Italy to employ the available working population leads, as has been seen, to massive migration to the North and abroad. If this situation cannot be altogether obviated, because of the costs involved or the limited ability of the South to develop its resources rapidly enough, the need will exist to reduce the difficulties associated with migration - to facilitate resettlement elsewhere and to cope with the problems that inward migration creates in the recipient areas.

In the United Kingdom, to take another example, the failure to provide sufficient jobs in the declining regions creates problems in other regions. To evaluate them, and to devise suitable strategies to deal with them necessitates an assessment of the effects of regional policies in the declining regions.

The same reasoning may, in other countries, lead to the decision to promote development in those regions which have the necessary conditions for it. The problems of regional imbalance can be dealt with in more than one way but the "right" strategy can only be chosen after considering the likely impact of the various policies which come into question.

Policies, objectives and methods, group (c) the third stage in a "systematic" approach to the formulation of regional strategies, after the relevant facts have been assembled and appraised, and the principles which govern selection of policies have been determined, is the actual choice of policies and the specific objectives and methods by which they can be implemented.

Here again, a distinction can be drawn between two kinds of regional strategies:

i) those strategies which are designed to affect the balance between regions, and

ii) those strategies which are designed to influence the development of individual regions.

The distinction is not a semantic one, but a practical one. It is based upon the fact firstly that interregional balance in any country is the outcome of the economic and social influences which bear upon the whole country - including regional policies themselves - but may bear differently on the individual regions. Secondly, on the fact that each region has its own individual characteristics, its size, population, economic structure, standard of living, socio-economic groups, urban and rural densities, environmental conditions, and so on.

In the jargon of regional policies this distinction is not always made, but it is an important one because the strategies and policies which are required for each are of a different character and affected by different considerations.

Distinction i) starts from the strategic decision itself that regionally differentiated policies, or discrimination between regions, is in fact necessary for national well being. This is not self-evident, for it is possible for any country to reach the conclusion that the national interest is best served by allowing, or requiring all regions to exist or compete with each other in equal terms. It is a decision which should be made consciously and deliberately, on the basis of evidence that the normal working of economic and social forces will not produce an acceptable situation.

This decision has of course already been reached in the majority of OECD countries, though not universally, and not to the same degree. It is certainly strongly held in Italy, the United Kingdom and Canada and has only comparatively recently become a tenet of national policy in Japan, and is perhaps least strongly held in the United States. In some other countries, such as the Federal Republic of Germany, the main reliance has been placed on the free working of the economic system and on the responsibility of each Land within the Federation to pursue its own development, with regional policies playing a relatively minor role. In France the important part played by the State in guiding the development of the country as a whole through, inter alia, a policy of Aménagement du Territoire automatically introduces a regional component in all national policies. In many other OECD countries a motivation for regional policies may lie in the unequal effects of economic change, as in Belgium, or the need for securing a better population distribution, as in Holland, etc.

Whatever may be the motivation for regionally differentiated policies, a further strategic decision is required to delimit the regions which are to be beneficiaries of discriminatory policies. Delimitation is necessary for two reasons. Firstly universal discrimination is a contradiction in terms; a country as a whole cannot, to put in bluntly, subsidize itself. Secondly, the larger the proportion of a country which is to benefit from regionally differentiated policies, the greater must be the resources required in proportion to the total available. Since they are, inevitably, limited, the extension of discriminatory policies in favour of larger and larger areas must weaken the effectiveness of the policies overall. The "national" regional strategy requires therefore some assessment of what can be afforded, in total, for discriminatory policies, and the effect they can have on the regional balance of the country as a whole.

This point deserves some emphasis in view of the fact, that, in many countries, the regions to which discriminatory policies apply may represent a half or more of the total population. If it is borne in mind that, regional policies are not the only form of discrimination and that other forms of special subventions or support (e. g. in agriculture, steel, coal, shipbuilding, textiles, not all of which are concentrated in particular regions), also present claims on national resources and are widely practised, the need to assess the limits which national resources place upon regional discriminatory policies becomes more than of academic importance.

The second "national" strategic decision is in the specific objectives and methods appropriate to these objectives. The specific objectives may be to increase the scale of the manufacturing industry in selected regions, or to develop new growth areas or population centres on the basis of a particular industrial structure. How far this can be achieved by, or necessitates, different types of measures, requires a realistic evaluation of the nature and scale of the problem and the effects that different types of measures can be expected to have in the given circumstances.

As regards ii) regional strategies – since each region has its own specific character the effectiveness of any policy for its development will depend on how well its needs and potential are surveyed and appraised. A "strategy" entails decisions on the specific areas within a region that are most capable of development, the deficiencies, in infrastructure, trained manpower or social institutions, that have to be remedied, and the capability the region has in attracting resources from outside – in capital, skilled manpower or services – which it cannot provide itself and are necessary for a sufficient rate of growth for its population. The differences between regions will dictate different strategies: in some the scope for development of manufacturing industry may be much greater than in others. In some the scope may be greater for improvements in infrastructure or the development of, say, tourism and office employment than in manufacture. It follows that the same measures, of "national" regional policy or of internal regional policy will produce different results in different regions, according to the differences in their structure and capability of development.

Since regions are not isolated, self contained parts of a country, but have a large degree of interdependence a regional strategy must be framed also with reference to its part in the complex web of inter-regional relationships which result from the fact that a country is, in a sense, an "organic" unity. Linkages between regions, through communications, and interconnected markets and sources of supply will accentuate the degree to which each region specializes in those industries and occupations in which it has a comparative advantage. The repercussion or multiplier effect of a stimulus to one region will spread beyond its boundaries, as will its contraction or restraint upon its development. To the extent that a regional strategy ignores this inter-dependence it may be both impracticable and lead to unexpected and possibly unwanted effects on other regions and the country as a whole.

The conclusions which emerge from this discussion are two fold. Firstly, that a number of "strategic" decisions have to be made before a rational choice can be made between the detailed methods (which will be considered in the next chapter) by which the strategies can be implemented. Secondly, that "national regional" strategies and those which relate to particular regions must be consistent with each other. Thus, the separate regional strategies which each provide for a given growth of manufacturing industry, will be unrealistic unless the sum total of the growth in each region corresponds with the national total. Similarly, regional strategies which envisage the elimination of net outward migration will not be consistent with other strategies which assume a continuance or increase in net inward migration.

The principles outlined in this chapter are by no means new or original. In drawing attention to them the Working Party is only summarizing the conclusions which it has drawn from the collective experience of the Member countries over a considerable period. This is not to say, however, that all countries have as yet fully applied these principles in working out their regional policies. Certainly some countries (notably France, Italy, Germany, Austria, Spain, Holland, Sweden and Norway) have gone to considerable lengths to set out both the framework of national policies and the regional strategies which they involve, in major policy documents. Of no one country, however, can it be said that there yet exists either the thoroughgoing analysis of regional problems, or a comprehensive evaluation of strategies which a systematic approach would require. The Working Party believes that many of the OECD countries would need to go further in this direction than they have done so far, if they are to find the "right" answer to their regional problems.

VI

THE METHODS AND INSTRUMENTS
OF REGIONAL POLICIES

In no respect is the experimental nature of regional policies more apparent than in the specific measures which Governments have employed in their pursuit. The frequency of changes has been a noticeable feature in the majority of countries. It reflects not only a changing appreciation of the problems themselves but also in views on the desirability and efficacy of particular methods. Changes occur not only when a new Government, with a different political philosophy from its predecessor takes office, but also during the life time of the same Government.

Frequency of change has its advantages and disadvantages. It is advantageous if it means that better methods supersede those which are ineffective, too costly in relation to their benefits or produce unwanted effects. It is disadvantageous when the new methods are no better than the old and when the measures are maintained for so short a time that reasoned judgement about their effects can hardly be formed. In the view of the Working Party the point has not been reached at which further experimentation can be dispensed with. At the same time the need is apparent for a greater degree of stability, if measures are to have their desired effects. This is however unlikely to be attained without an attempt to determine as dispassionately as possible, the merits and demerits of particular methods and the circumstances in which they are likely to be effective for their purpose.

It would clearly be impossible, within the confines of a short report, to examine and appraise in detail all the methods used by OECD countries and the way they have influenced the regional situation. Where collective, international, experience may be of value is in the examination of those questions of principle which arise in choosing between a variety of methods, in assessing the part they can play in attaining policy objectives or in appraising their wider implications.

91

This is the approach adopted by the Working Party in its studies and this chapter sets out the main conclusions it has reached.

Types of Measures

The types of measures can be classified in more than one way and individual measures can come within more than one category. As a first approximation the following classification gives some indication of the range of measures which are to be found among OECD countries:

1)   Financial incentives to industry.

2)   Restraints on expansion.

3)   The promotion of infrastructure.

4)   Manpower policies.

5)   Planned and co-ordinated development.

6)   Public finance policies.

7)   Institutional and organisational change.

8)   Location of Central Government Services and of Government procurement contracts.

These types of measures may be used singly or in combination with each other. Most countries use some or all of them in combination, a fact which provides at least one lesson of common experience, namely, that regional policies call for more than one type of measure and that finding the right general strategy is partly a question of deciding how much reliance to place on each of them. It also suggests that the effectiveness of any one type of measure may depend on the adoption of complementary measures and cannot be assessed in isolation from that of the complementary measures.

Criteria for Judgement of Regional Policy Measures

One of the difficulties in discussing measures of these types in terms of regional policies is that they are also the means by which more general aims are pursued. Thus incentives to industry are given in many countries to promote investment generally, or to support particular industries deemed to be of special importance in the national economy. Restraints on expansion are required for purposes of physical planning, to ensure the coordinated development of town and country, and a rational allocation of land in its different uses,

housing, industry and commerce, communications and amenities.
Manpower policies, training, retraining, and resettlement are required
to enable workers to adapt to the changing techniques, technical skills
and demands of industry. The promotion of infrastructure is required
for constant renewal and development of the physical and social
equipment - roads, railways, ports, water, schools, universities,
hospitals, etc. , which are necessary for the life of the community.
Public finance policies are required for the management of the economy,
for allocating resources between the public and private sectors and
for the promotion of different kinds of development in accordance with
urgency of need and priorities.

It is therefore only insofar as these types of measures are applied
with specific regional objectives in mind that they can be properly
designated as measures of regional policy. The criterion by which
both the need for such measures, and the effect they are likely to have
can be judged, is their ability to modify the regional effects of the
general policies of the same type. It follows that when the general
policies themselves are pursued with regional objectives in mind, the
need for specific regional measures will be lessened; and that when the
general policies are pursued without reference to regional objectives
and are the main determinant in the allocation of resources the effect
of the specific regional measures will be correspondingly lessened.

These points are worth making since there is an all too common
tendency in most countries to judge the value of regional measures, and
the need to alter or strengthen them, without reference to the working
of the more general policies on the regional problems themselves.
It is a constant, underlying, theme of this report that specific regional
and 'national' policies cannot be considered in isolation from each
other. Both bear on the regional situation as a whole and it is only
when their joint influence is evaluated that it is possible to make
reasoned judgements on the usefulness or otherwise of specific regional
measures.

Even after allowing for the influence of national policies on the
regional situation the problem of deciding what tests should be applied
in judging the merits of specific regional measures remains a difficult
one. Too exclusive attention to one criterion, to the neglect of others,
is a fault which can easily lead to the wrong measures, or to the
wrong balance between different types of measures by which regional
policies can be implemented.

For example, financial incentives to promote industrial growth in
a particular region will satisfy the test of effectiveness if growth is
actually promoted or decline avoided. This may not, however,
justify their adoption if (a) growth would have occurred without the

measures (b) the cost of the measures is disproportionate to the amount
of growth achieved (c) the wrong kind of industrial growth is stimulat-
ed (d) the growth produces detrimental effects on industry elsewhere
and international trade (e) could have been achieved by other measures
at less cost or with more beneficial effects in other respects.

Similarly, measures for planned development of new or existing
towns as an alternative to excessive growth of congested conurbations
may be deemed 'effective' if the development actually occurs. But
they may not be the 'right' measures (a) if they are so costly in
resources as to require a cut back in other, equally desirable
directions (b) if there is a lack of balance in growth of population and
employment opportunities, causing either unemployment in the
expanding towns or excessive travel to work and commuting (c) if
infrastructure costs are so high in the early years as to add more to
the costs of industry than would have been the case if other locations
had been chosen for development.

Measures to develop infrastructure may also be effective when,
for example, roads are built to improve communications between main
centres or between main and local centres. They may, however,
have unintended or unexpected results, stimulating the economy in the
larger centres with a sufficient economic base to take advantage of
better access to markets and weakening the industries in the smaller
centres which become more accessible to the larger scale manufacturers (a phenomenon which has in fact occurred as a result of
improvement in national communications in a number of countries
such as the United States and Italy).

One other difficulty in attempting to judge the merits of particular
regional policy measures should also be mentioned. This is that they
work differently in different circumstances. In Chapter IV it has been
noted that there are many factors at work which influence the regional
balance of a country. They also affect the working of regional policy
measures themselves, sometimes nullifying them, sometimes
creating conditions which are favourable to their working.

To take one example, the upswings and downswings of the economy
exercise a strong influence on the results that can be achieved by
regional policy measures. In the upswing the pressure of demand may
lead to the full absorption of existing industrial capacity and the
available labour in some regions before it does in others. In the
downswing both capacity and labour may be under-utilized in all regions.
In both sets of circumstances the same regional policy measures will
have quite different effects. In the upswing such regional incentives
or restraints as there are may be sufficient, or more than sufficient,
to accentuate the national tendency to expand elsewhere than in the

regions which are already working to full capacity. In the downswing the same incentives and restraints may be less than sufficient, or quite insufficient to offset the causes of the downswing or to stimulate any investment at all in any of the regions if the overall economic 'climate' is unfavourable to it.

It will be seen therefore that a number of general points need to be borne in mind in any consideration of the merits of different types of regional measures. For convenience they are summarized as follows:

1) The working of each type of method is influenced by the existence or absence of complementary measures of other types.

2) They operate differently, according to the influence of national policies and the factors which affect the course of the national economy.

3) The merits of individual types of measures can be judged in terms of several rather than one criterion: these include (a) the direct results in relation to their costs (b) the comparative advantage of one method over another in ability to secure the same results (c) the indirect results, beneficial or otherwise and intended or not.

It follows that a priori judgements as to what will constitute the "best" method or "best" choice of measures for dealing with regional problems are unlikely to have much validity. Only if sufficient weight is given to the circumstances in which they are to operate and to the criteria by which their effects can be judged, can an adequate basis be found for selecting one rather than another type of measure or any combination of measures. This conclusion is of some importance. It reinforces what has already been said in the previous chapter in relation to strategies. The improvement of regional policies and rendering them more effective will depend on the progress that can be made towards a systematic evaluation both of the relevant background circumstances and of the criteria by which specific measures should be judged.

In the remainder of this chapter we examine some of the issues that are raised in relation to individual measures, having regard to the foregoing general considerations.

Incentives for Industry

In the majority of the countries one of the main instruments of regional policy is the provision of specific financial inducements to private enterprises to encourage establishment or expansion, maintenance or avoidance of contraction of certain types of industry in selected regions or locations. It is a measure of regional policy par excellence, since its primary purpose is to bring about a different geographical distribution of industry from that which could be expected without the inducements. In terms of budgetary funds expended it probably constitutes the largest single item in the armoury of specifically regional measures.

The following table (page 97) indicates the gross amounts (in $ US) spent in a recent period and, where estimates have been made, planned to be spent in the future.

In each country the areas to which the inducements apply reflect the specific aims of regional policy. In Italy they are primarily designed to benefit the backward Mezzogiorno; in the United Kingdom the "development" and "intermediate" areas of relatively high unemployment or comparative stagnation; in France, Spain, Japan and other countries in areas not only of economic weaknesses (high unemployment or low incomes) but in areas selected for expansion in accordance with planned development policies. This distinction is of some significance since it indicates that incentive measures are used not only to counteract economic weakness but also to promote expansion as a desirable end in itself.

The industries which may benefit are mainly in manufacture, on the - somewhat unproved - basis that it is manufacture which provides the main generating and trigger or multiplier effects on employment and development generally. They may, however, include some "service" industries such as tourism and hotel development and office development and other tertiary sector activities. They are increasingly being extended to such activities, e. g. recently in France, as it is becoming apparent that the theory that services follow industry is losing its validity.

The specific types of inducements are numerous, and in most countries more than one type is used. Broadly, they come within the following classes:

1) Grants for equipment, plant and machinery.

2) Provision of factory buildings and development sites at low cost.

TOTAL VALUE OF REGIONAL INCENTIVES OF DIRECT
BENEFIT TO INDIVIDUAL ENTERPRISES

(In million US $ at current prices
and current exchange rates)

COUNTRY	ANNUAL EXPENDITURE	FORESEEN ANNUAL EXPENDITURE
Belgium	1971: 95.4	..
Canada	Fiscal 1969/70: 52	Fiscal 1974/75: 119
Denmark	Fiscal 1970/71: 2.3	..
Finland	1972: 3.9	1974: 40.8
France	1972: 71.9	..
Germany F.R.	1971: 206.1	..
Ireland	Fiscal 1969/70: 53.6	Fiscal 1974/75: 121
Italy	1970: 295.4	..
Netherlands	Average 1964/72: 13.8	..
Norway	Average 1968/72: 10.4	..
Spain.............................	Average 1964/70: 4.2	..
Sweden	Fiscal 1972/73: 26.8	..
United Kingdom	Average $\frac{1967/68}{1971/72}$: 592.8	Average $\frac{1972/73}{1976/77}$: 766.8

NOTE: The expenditure data comprise the following elements:

Belgium : Interest subsidies.

Canada : Investment grants.

Denmark : Investment grants. Over the 5 years 1967/71 total grants and loans amounted to ca. US $ 53 million. These are expected to rise to US $ 100 million in the 5 years 1972/76.

Finland : Interest subsidies and, for 1974, compensation for the employment of inexperienced labour.

France : Regional development grants, decentralization assistance.

Germany F.R. : 269 million DM (budget data in the Federal Budget). This figure does not include other kinds of regional aids (e.g., tax reductions, ERP loans). The expenditures of the Laender are not available for this period. In 1969 a new instrument of regional aid was set up in the form of tax exempt investment grants. These are provided by local tax authorities out of current tax revenues. These grants are not shown in the Budget. The short-fall in tax revenues in 1971 was estimated as being 486 million DM. This has been included in the figure shown on the table.

Ireland : Investment grants.

Italy : Investment grants, interest subsidies (excluding those specially given to small and medium sized businesses).

Netherlands : Investment grants.

Norway : Direct grants (commitments). These amounted to 369.3 million Kr over the period 1968-72. Over this period loans and guarantees for loans (commitments) amounted to 1,802 million Kr. These are not included in the table.

Spain : Investment grants in the development poles.

Sweden : Investment grants, employment premiums, interest subsidies.

United Kingdom : Expenditure on regional incentives of direct benefit to individual enterprises by the United Kingdom Government, net of loan repayments and factory rents and sales.

3)   Loans at market or specially favourable rates of interest, as a contribution towards capital costs.

4)   Reduced taxation on profits over a period.

5)   Favourable rates of amortization of capital expenditure for tax purposes.

6)   Favourable tax treatment of revenue from state aids.

7)   Reduction or elimination of state charges, local taxes, licence fees, etc.

8)   Alleviation of certain costs, e. g. social security contributions, transport charges where these are within state control.

9)   Grants towards labour costs. *

The incentives are normally applied under legislation specifying the duration of the period in which they are to be available, either indefinite or time-limited. The legislation will also specify the conditions to be fulfilled by the beneficiaries. Of importance is the question of whether they are available automatically to all enterprises within specified categories in the region or area to which the incentives apply, or selectively on the discretion of the administrating authority in accordance with specified conditions which link the granting of incentives with undertakings from the enterprise (such as its own contribution of capital or to employment).

Over time experience leads countries to change their systems of incentives, abandoning some and adopting others, and also to change the areas to which they apply. It also leads them to change the size of individual incentives from time to time, increasing or decreasing the proportion that they may bear to the total costs of the individual enterprise.

The Annex gives a summary picture of the incentives which are currently in force in each country. Direct comparisons between scales and rates of individual incentives are, however, likely to be misleading since it is the totality of all the incentives available and their relevance to the cost structures of enterprises that can provide any meaningful comparison. Most countries also have different taxation systems, so that the net value of incentives or relief after tax will be different from the gross value before tax. In addition, the qualifying conditions vary between countries, so that more stringent conditions may offset what are apparently higher incentives. Moreover,

---

*   E. g. regional employment premium in the United Kingdom, employment grants introduced in 1970 in a limited area in Sweden.

98

the Annex relates only to central Government expenditures and omits local government expenditures for similar purposes which are very important in some countries.

Nonetheless calculations can be made to show that incentives individually or taken together, may represent a substantial proportion of a firm's costs. Estimates that have been made show, for example, that in Canada, Ireland and Italy (Mezzogiorno), the current incentives may be worth up to half a firm's capital expenditure and in France (west and south-west) and in Germany (zonal border areas) up to one quarter.

Any consideration of the principles involved in the use of financial incentives to promote industrial development in certain regions, in preference to others, can therefore start from the facts that the incentives can and usually do make a substantial impact on the cost structures of the beneficiary enterprises. It is necessary, however, to go beyond this basic fact and to consider how far incentives are capable of influencing the regional distribution of industry and what other consequences they may have.

On the first point there is ample evidence from the experience of OECD countries to show that the decisions of some enterprises are positively swayed by the availability of incentives. In the United Kingdom, Southern Italy, Belgium, France, to mention only some, industries and plants exist in the preferential regions which might well not exist without the incentives. To this extent, incentives can be regarded as a necessary and useful tool of regional policy but there are a number of factors which suggest that there are limitations to what can be achieved by incentives alone.

Firstly, other factors exercise a considerable influence on the decisions of enterprises as to location of new establishments or expansion of existing plants. Surveys have been carried out in the United Kingdom, Italy, the United States and elsewhere which show that access to markets and to suppliers of raw materials and components, availability of management and labour of various skills, water and energy, suitable sites, housing and social services and amenities for workers together with environmental quality all have an influence. These factors affect not only the immediate require-ments of an enterprise but condition its operational efficiency and viability over its lifetime, and its ability to stand up to competition from equally efficient and well located producers elsewhere. Decisions about location and scale of production are among the most important an enterprise can take. Unless its various needs can be satisfied throughout its foreseeable future, its decisions are unlikely to be swayed by the single factor of incentives alone.

The fact that the duration of incentives of various kinds is uncertain, since Government policies may change, also limits the influence of incentives on investment decisions. Insofar as an enterprise treats incentives as a "once for all" benefit, and discounts for uncertainty those that might be available in the future, the overall influence of the incentives on the longer term decisions of the enterprise will be reduced.

Secondly, incentives work in favour of "preferred" regions or areas only when they confer a sufficient differential advantage. The absolute size of the incentives is no measure of their differential, since this is determined both by the prelavent conditions outside the preferred regions and by the systems of taxation and financial reliefs and incentives which affect investment in them. Thus a reduction in corporate taxes throughout the country, or a change in the reliefs for the amortization of capital, without a corresponding change in regional incentives will alter the differential value of the incentives. Moreover, if the incentives do not adequately compensate for the locational disadvantages that may exist in the preferred regions their effect will be correspondingly reduced.

Thirdly, the question of "mobility" of industry, its ability to change location, is of crucial importance in determining the effectiveness of incentive systems. Clearly, some capacity for mobility exists in all countries. But most firms grow from small beginnings and once a firm is established, both its needs for new locations and its ability to develop elsewhere become more limited. The maintenance of its managerial and labour force, its linkages with markets and suppliers predispose towards remaining where it is. In such circumstances it will change its location, or engage in expansion elsewhere only if the advantages are such as to outweigh the costs of moving, including those resulting from any interruption of its normal productive rhythm.

Incentives may, however, play a part in tipping the balance towards movement. Nonetheless experience in most countries indicates that there are inherent difficulties in bringing about a significant, large scale switch in the geographical distribution of a country's industries, and that no system of incentives so far, however large they may seem, can be expected to exercise more than a marginal influence on the general, geographical, distribution of industries. The bulk of a country's industries, particularly mining and manufacturing, is located where historical factors have caused it to be, in and around the main centres of population which provide both its markets and source of manpower of all kinds. Many enterprises are small in scale, tied to their familiar and traditional locations. Larger firms with plants in more than one region and with greater capital resources are

100

the principle source of 'mobile' industry but are still severly conditioned by the factors which determined their original location.

Of more importance, however, is the fact that the overall growth of industry in general, and of manufacturing industry in particular, is marginal and liable to fluctuations. An average annual growth in a country's total output of goods and services of, say X% does not of itself produce a need for a corresponding enlargement in its capital equipment or factory space. It is largely brought about by improved utilization of equipment and buildings, more efficient productive methods and the substitution of newer and better machinery for obsolete types. Even, therefore, comparatively high rates of output growth produce only marginal increments of totally new establishments, and a marginal increment in the total labour force required by them. In periods of contracting national output - in the downswing of the economy - contractions and closures are more frequent and lessen still further the amount of available mobile industry. The power of incentives to cause a substantial change in the regional distribution of industry should not, therefore, be over estimated, in periods of upswing and downswing alike. Also, the wider the areas or regions in which the incentives are available, the less is likely to be each region's share of the total 'mobile' industry that is available.

It should also not be overlooked that mobility may be in more than one direction. Existing enterprises in "preferred" or incentive regions may be motivated by their basic economics to move away from them despite the incentives. Amalgamation, mergers and reorganisation of enterprises operating nationally or in several regions may dictate the closing, or contraction of plants in preferred regions, despite the incentives. The increasing scale of organisation and tendency to integration works in more than one way, so that incentive systems may sometimes do little more than reinforce the total financial positions of an enterprise, without materially affecting its location pattern.

Finally, reference should be made to the character of the industries which may be affected by incentives. Two distinctions can be drawn; between locally based and external industries and between "capital intensive" and "labour intensive" industries.

In the majority of OECD countries the various incentives for industries in particular regions are usually available both to industries already existing in the region or moving into it. Insofar, however, as the conditions in the incentive regions are unfavourable to local enterprise, e. g. through lack of experience, knowledge and connections with established markets the incentives will stimulate local enterprise only if adequate complementary measures are successfully undertaken, a difficult process, however, if there is not already a sufficient industrial and commercial base for them. External enterprise can, however, bring its experience, etc. to the incentive region, so that, initially at least, if incentives work at all, they are likely to increase the role of external enterprise. This will be advantageous if it, in fact, provides a stimulus to local enterprise and has a longer term "trigger effect" on the development of the region. This does not always happen as experience in Southern Italy, and, to some extent, in the United Kingdom has shown. If it does not happen, the increased dependence of a region on externally based industries may not be altogether advantageous. Development may be overconcentrated in the areas which are particularly attractive to them, to the detriment of general development, and the net revenues of the external industries accrue to their owners outside the region, without providing a source of suitable secondary and tertiary industrial growth. Externally based growth is, no doubt, preferable to none at all but it is beginning to be accepted in several countries that regional development will only be properly balanced if local as well as external enterprise is able to participate. This in itself indicates the need to evaluate incentive policies from this standpoint.

The bulk of the incentives that have been listed are, basically, contributions to the capital rather than operational expenses of an enterprise, to equipment, sites and buildings, rather than running costs. This is not the same as saying that they only assist "capital intensive" industries since they can also contribute significantly to the overall costs of more "labour intensive" industries which still require equipment and buildings, etc. Nonetheless they do contribute to the former and insofar as the result of incentives is to attract to the regions concerned a larger number of capital intensive industries the benefit of those industries in terms of absorption of local labour is reduced. This is a factor of particular importance where the main objective of regional policy is to increase employment opportunities as such.

The inference cannot be drawn, however, that, even in such cases, incentives should be concentrated on those which directly stimulate employment. Modern industry is itself increasingly capital intensive and it may serve little purpose to stimulate more intensive use of labour if this leads to inefficient or uncompetitive production methods. On the other hand, unless the incentive system is geared to promoting industries which increase demand for labour they may not have their desired effect on the employment situation. In the light of the experience of many countries the Working Party believes that more attention should be given by Governments to this aspect when reviewing their industrial incentive policies.

The Role of Incentives

The foregoing section shows that the evaluation of the effects of incentives is a difficult task and that their effectiveness depends not only on their nature and scale but on the existence of the complementary conditions necessary for the development the incentives are designed to encourage. Thus they are likely to be more effective, for example, if they are well geared to the needs of the industrial enterprises they assist, if the general economic climate is conducive to expansion and to the generation of a sufficient volume of mobile industry able to locate itself in the regions requiring special measures and if adequate steps are taken to remedy deficiencies in manpower skills and training or in infrastructure which may exist in the regions concerned.

This being said, it should be stressed that incentives themselves play a fundamental part in regional policies, insofar as their aim is to correct those conditions in a structurally weak or backward region which, in a world of competition prevent them playing their full part in the national economy. Basically they aim to compensate for certain disadvantages of various kinds (insufficient local capital and enterprise, poverty, backwardness, insufficient trained manpower, poor infrastructure, etc.), and thereby to render the regions concerned more able to compete with other regions. Disadvantaged regions, especially those remote from or on the periphery of, the national economy may suffer from higher costs of production as a result of their disadvantages, so that incentives may serve to offset or compensate for such disadvantages. To the extent that they do so they serve to create a greater parity of conditions between regions and bring the disadvantaged regions into a position in which they are able to compete effectively with other regions. This is particularly important in countries where a major effort is needed to enable extensive under-developed regions to participate more fully in the development of the country as a whole within a framework of an essentially competitive economy. There are also various examples of countries in which large regions, peripheral to the main centres of economic development, suffer from historical factors leading to structural weaknesses or decline. In this process the effective use of incentives must be regarded as a fundamental necessity.

The Working Party does not doubt therefore that incentive systems, suitably devised, have an essential part to play in the implementation of regional policies.

Though incentives have this fundamental and positive role it is also legitimate to recognize that concern is sometimes expressed that incentive policies may be pushed too far. The argument here is that,

even when incentives are effective in promoting economic expansion
in the disadvantaged regions they may do so at an excessive net cost
to national economic growth. This possibility cannot be easily
evaluated. On the one hand incentives may stimulate investment in
enterprises which (without the incentives) yield a lower return on the
total capital invested than could be obtained if it were invested elsewhere. If private costs only are taken into account there would be a
net loss in national returns on capital, and if private costs and
returns are considered in isolation there might be a reduction in the
aggregate return on capital in the country as a whole. On the other
hand, private and social costs and returns often diverge. Indeed it is
a basic argument in favour of incentives that they are necessary to
compensate for the relatively high social costs to the community
which do not enter into the calculation of the individual enterprises.

It is certainly not possible to be dogmatic and to assert that
incentive policies need necessarily lead to a net loss to the community.
Whether they will do so must depend on how private and social costs
are evaluated.

The fact that incentives may produce a net loss is not always
apparent, since the benefitting enterprises may themselves be made
more profitable as a result of the incentives and the corresponding
disbenefits to the nation in the shape of alternative development
foregone cannot be seen.

Such 'disbenefits' can nonetheless occur. Incentives may enable
industries to survive, for a time, while maintaining inefficient
structures and methods. They can reduce the stimulus that
competition brings to adaptation, enabling enterprises to postpone
necessary measures to improve their efficiency and competitiveness.
At the same time other, more efficient enterprises, which are not
in areas qualifying for incentives, may have insufficient capital for
their needs (a solution which in part may result from the level of
taxation required to support inefficient industries). "Automatic"
systems of incentives have the advantage of more widespread application
than selective and discretionary systems but they may confer benefits
on inefficient and efficient firms alike. Unless ways are found to
combine incentives with measures to secure competitive efficiency they
can lead to no lasting improvement and the industries that have been
supported by incentive measures become at risk when the incentives
cease, and the prospect of Governments being able at some stage to
dispense with incentives and to rely on selfsustaining regional development becomes remote.

It should be recognized also that incentives, though benefitting
individual enterprises, do not thereby necessarily contribute either to

regional employment or development. For example, an existing firm in an incentive region may receive X% of the cost of a particular piece of capital equipment which it might well have installed from its own resources. Whether it will use the incentive funds to increase its total investment, or its profits, dividends or reserves, or expand its output and employment, depends on its judgement of its whole situation. There can be little doubt that many of the "automatic" incentives in a number of countries, whether on capital equipment or labour, have in fact been absorbed by individual firms without appreciably affecting either their overall position or their major decisions on output, employment or expansion. Insofar as this has happened, a large part of the expenditure on incentives must be regarded as a simple financial transfer to regional production and employment. This is particularly true when the general economic climate is unfavourable to expansion.

Against this, it can be argued that the incentives at least pump money into a region and help to retain a higher degree of profitability than would otherwise be the case. There is some force in this argument, which favours the use of automatic incentives as a counter-cyclical anti-depression measure. But it is not necessarily an argument in favour of automatic incentives as a means of curing the underlying and persistent causes of regional backwardness and decline, or of steering industry to areas selected for expansion under a national strategy.

In some countries payments from regional incentive measures represent a sizeable and often growing proportion of total investment. National growth rates have however sometimes been high in countries which have made little use of regional incentives and low in others which have used them on a significant scale. Too much should not be attributed to the fact that the United Kingdom which has devoted more resources to regional incentives than any other country has also had one of the slowest growth rates. This has many causes which are outside the scope of this report, but it serves to highlight the need to consider the effects of incentives not only on the regions to which they apply but on the development of the economy as a whole.

Restraints on Expansion

Restraints have been a tool of regional policy in several countries. Leaving aside those which are required for local planning purposes the main examples are the use of licensing systems on industrial and office building in the United Kingdom, the French system of licensing and special taxes operating in the Paris region and more recent

105

attempts on similar lines in the Netherlands, Italy and Japan. Sweden has established a system of prior consultations without controls or penalties. The theory behind such systems is partly that they reduce the pressure of demand on resources in "overheated" and "congested" regions or in areas within them, and partly that they encourage development elsewhere.

The experience of those countries which have used such measures over any length of time, particularly in the United Kingdom and France, has been varied and has not hitherto been such as to permit very definite conclusions to be drawn. It is a subject on which the Working Party intends to give further study. In the United Kingdom restraints have been applied with varying degrees of severity, more intensively in past periods of upswing. There is evidence that they were effective in obliging certain industries to choose locations in the development areas and that at various times they were a useful means of ensuring that firms properly considered the possibilities of location in those areas before reaching a decision. Some commentators have argued that the system had entailed losses to the economy rather than gains, by forcing firms away from locations of their choice to others which were disadvantageous to them and detrimental to their ability to compete with firms in other countries which could freely choose their own locations. In the more recent past the controls have been relaxed by raising the minimum levels of factory floor space for which a licence is required in the South and West Midlands and eliminating the need for licenses altogether in other regions. This occurred near the bottom of a recession and reflected the need for a general increase in industrial investment and a greater reliance on incentives and new organisational measures in the development regions. At the same time controls on office development were also lifted except for the South East Region. In both the United Kingdom and France the controls have been used not to ban development but to restrain it. While the controls can have a greater influence on "mobile" industry than on industry that is tied to a congested region the policy has had some success in limiting expansion e.g. in manufacturing industry in the Paris region. By contrast it has had little influence in limiting expansion of the tertiary sector in that region, or of promoting dispersal of office employment from the South East to the depressed regions in the United Kingdom.

Judgement on whether restraint systems are needed can only be made in the light of the particular circumstance of individual countries. A number of countries, such as the Netherlands, Italy and Japan are experimenting with stronger measures to restrain development in congested regions or regions of high growth. In the United Kingdom recent policies have placed more emphasis on incentives than on restraints, though the system itself remains operative. Countries such as the United States and Germany have relied on the working of market

forces rather than on restraints as a means of securing a different
distribution of economic activity. The diversity of practices among
countries and the difficulty of assessing results of restraint systems
where they have been tried preclude arriving at any very firm
conclusions. It could be argued that restraint in one region does not
of itself promote expansion in others unless conditions in general
are favourable to such expansion and the restraints cannot be evaded.
Beyond this it would seem difficult to go.

The Promotion of Infrastructure

All OECD countries that are pursuing regional policies appear
to recognize that the promotion of infrastructure is essential to them.
This applies in countries where the regional problem is that of
"backward" regions which have not so far been able to participate in
the general progress of the nation: in countries where new and modern
industries must take the place of declining staple industries and in
those in which regional policy aims at developing new growth areas as
part of a comprehensive national development programme. Without
the necessary communications, roads, air and sea ports, energy and
water supplies, housing and health, and education facilities, industry
and commerce cannot flourish. Financial incentives alone do not
compensate for deficiencies in infrastructure, but the development of
infrastructure will enable the incentives to have more effect, in
attracting external enterprises to the regions concerned or in generating
enterprises. There is little doubt, from the experience of OECD
countries, that the promotion of infrastructure is a vital task of regional
policies.

Such general statements, however, provide no guide to the question
of how far should the development of infrastructure be pressed, in
comparison with other measures, and what forms of infrastructure are
most likely to contribute to the aims of particular regional policies.
Investment in infrastructure of various kinds is not only necessary but
is one of the largest claimants on national resources. Since these are
limited, a choice has to be made between alternative uses. This applies
as much in the regional policy field as in others and the effectiveness
and justification of regional infrastructure policies will depend on how
that choice is exercised.

A basic advantage of infrastructure development in any region is
that, assuming maintenance, it is permanent in its effect. Roads, etc.,
once built, are there for the future generations and are foundations
on which future economic activity and growth can be built. They do not,
however, create such activity, or lead to growth unless they conform

with the predisposing conditions for them. Roads in unpopulated regions do not bring population to them if they are too remote or otherwise unsuited to development. The improvement of infrastructure in already populated areas will make little difference to their economic growth if the existing infrastructure is already sufficient for the industries which can be sustained in them; or if the improvements are not sufficient to offset the disadvantages of the areas compared with other areas.

The time scale over which infrastructure policies can take effect will also be an important consideration. A vital bridge or the removal of a communication bottleneck may have an immediate effect. The construction of a road network may both take years to complete and not have its full effect until complementary development - energy supplies, water, housing, schools and industries - has also taken place.

Infrastructure development is a necessary part of the general development process at work throughout a country. It is possible to speak of a regional infrastructure policy when it implies some form of preferential treatment for particular regions, either in the allocation of the funds that are available for infrastructure development or by the modification, in favour of selected regions, of the principles by which they are allocated. On the other hand, the development of the same regions may be affected as such, or more, by improvement in the national infrastructure which may require development elsewhere. In the long term the completion of a national network of roads, an electricity Grid or certain ports and harbours may bring more benefit to peripheral, declined or backward regions than preferential measures within the region itself. Diversion of resources away from urgent national needs may sometimes work to the disadvantage of the regions which are given preferential treatment.

One method of regional infrastructure policy is to modify the criteria for investment decisions in favour of the preferred regions, e.g. by requiring a lower net return, however, this may be measured, than in other regions. In other words that investment in infrastructure can have a significant promotional effect on development of the weaker regions. Thus the general criterion that a major road should be built when there is an expectation of a given traffic load, or when it could relieve other roads to a specified degree, may be modified to permit construction in a preferred region on less stringent conditions. Such modifications may be made on the general principle that development of the preferred regions is so necessary, in political and social terms, that ordinary cost/benefit criteria should not be too vigorously applied. They can be made also in the belief that the infrastructure development can lead indirectly to economic development which cannot be measured in the narrow cost/benefit formulae of traffic loads, etc.

The studies of various cost/benefit techniques made by the Working Party* suggest that they do not always sufficiently allow for the indirect benefits which are often difficult to assess. The extent to which modifications of general criteria are justified by the need for the development of the preferred regions must remain largely a matter of judgement, fortified by close appraisal of the local circumstances.

The complete abandonment of cost/benefit techniques for deciding how far to promote infrastructure in the regions of preference would however have certain consequences. When the preference regions constitute a large part of a country - as they do - the use of scarce resources becomes increasingly arbitrary and the danger is augmented that they will be less effectively applied than they could be to the problems of the whole country. Secondly, they can lead to the application of other criteria which are even more unsatisfactory, such as differences between regions in the "ratio" of their infrastructure area, population, etc. Such rules of thumb ignore both the differing real needs of each region for infrastructure development and the real effect that improvements can produce. Rather than abandon cost/benefit techniques altogether, and resort to greater arbitrariness, it would seem better to revise them to ensure that they are more capable of evaluating the indirect benefit that specific measures for infrastructure development can bring to the regions.

The responsibility for infrastructure development in most countries is not centralized. Central Government, local and regional authorities, statutory bodies and, in some cases, private enterprise share the responsibility. Each will operate within its own framework of policy and criteria for the use of its resources. These can be modified for the purposes of regional policy and in many OECD countries this is increasingly done by the provision of central Government funds to the other bodies, or by modification of the rules under which they operate. Since the various types of infrastructure are complementary to each other the effectiveness of a regional infrastructure policy will largely be determined by the degree of co-ordination between the responsible authorities.

It is difficult to convey a precise statistical picture of expenditure on infrastructure for regional purposes, since in many countries no separation is made between this and expenditure for ordinary purposes.

The Working Party fully endorses the view that improvement of infrastructure has a vital part to play in all regional policies, and will largely determine the effectiveness of other measures. This does not,

*   See "Cost-Effectiveness Analysis and Regional Development", OECD, 1971.

however, mean disregard of the ordinary economic principle that investment can be justified only by the results that may be expected from it, measured against the costs involved, including alternative development that must be foregone. There is clearly a need in applying cost/benefit techniques to ensure that indirect as well as direct benefits that flow from infrastructure development should be assessed. No general, or rule of thumb, principles can be a substitute for careful evaluation, in particular regional circumstances, of what infrastructure development can be expected to achieve in the shape of economic growth.

Manpower Policies

Regional problems pose manpower problems in a number of ways. In 'backward' regions the root of backwardness is not only in the lack of physical resources and industries but the insufficient level of human ability, conditioned both by lack of education and opportunities for acquiring skills. In regions of declining industries new skills must be acquired suited to the industries that take their place. In regions for expansion, manpower will be needed in increasing numbers, in proportion to the economic development that takes place and in accordance with its character. Migration may be an essential element in regional policies or unavoidable.

There are several different elements in regional manpower policies:

1) The improvement of basic and higher education, in the regions in which it is lacking.

2) Vocational and technical training suited to the industries which are, or will be in the regions.

3) Resettlement and relocation of people who are, or will be unable, to find employment in their own regions or areas (because of, or despite, regional policies).

Each of these, but especially 1) and 2) come within the normal social policies in all countries. The need for specific regional measures arises when the normal policies fail to generate a sufficient level of education and training to permit the desired economic growth. Thus educational systems which are financed largely from local resources will be less able to provide the schools, colleges and training facilities in poorer than in more prosperous regions. This problem does not arise when national systems of education are financed by 'equalization' schemes which provide additional resources for poorer regions.

Vocational and technical training may be done within industry but, if the industrial base is too small, or not wide ranging enough, supplementary facilities will be necessary, and more so in some regions than in others.

Such problems have engaged the attention of Governments, OECD and other international organisations over a long period. It is appropriate to stress the need to consider them in their regional as well as more general national context. The concentration of regional policies on incentives and physical development can itself sometimes lead to an under-emphasis of the need for adequate education and training policies and to a misjudgement of what can be achieved, by the introduction of new industries for which the available manpower is not suited. Without measures for education and training, the resources spent on other measures of regional policy may fail to benefit those for whom it is primarily designed.

Resettlement and Relocation

The need to settle people in new locations arises, whichever of the two alternative principles of regional manpower policies are followed - "work to the workers" or "workers to the work". In the former case, regional policies may be insufficient to generate a sufficient movement of industry to provide employment where people are; and in the latter it is an aim of policy itself to encourage movement of people to where the employment opportunities can most effectively be provided.

How far special measures are required to facilitate the matching of people to employment opportunities, in whatever part of a country these may become available, is a factual matter and can only be assessed in relation to the concrete circumstances in a country. Much movement and relocation occurs from personal initiative and the willingness of people to seek a better life elsewhere and to face and overcome such difficulties and obstacles as may present themselves. In most countries voluntary migration and resettlement still accounts for the bulk of the local and interregional migration that occurs. Some of it is inevitable and even desirable. The problem for regional policy is to ensure that it actually takes place to the extent that it is an inescapable and necessary part of adjustment to new conditions or planned development and that the attendant social problems are minimized so far as possible.

It entails firstly making sure that people have adequate information about employment opportunities elsewhere, and the capacity of the areas to meet their needs in terms of housing, transport and social

services. The extension of the services given by local employment
offices or agencies to cover information on conditions outside their
own localities should be regarded as a necessary measure for bringing
manpower supply and demand into balance throughout a country in
accordance with the actual state of regional development (rather than
a theoretically desirable state which does not materialize).

Secondly, it entails reducing the obstacles to necessary movement.
The most important of these are the costs of transfer to a new location,
and the initial loss of income during periods of seeking new employment, or of retraining in new occupations. Such cost acts as a
deterrent to movement. If the obstacles are not recognized and reduced,
the result may be to retain people in areas where they cannot satisfactorily meet their needs for employment or an adequate standard of
living, while underutilizing the ability of other areas in which they could.

The counterpart of a policy designed to facilitate movement is that
adequate provision should also be made in the recipient areas for
social needs, for accomodation, education, health and welfare services.
This is important in areas of planned growth, if population is to
increase pari passu with the growth of industry. It is important also
in areas which have the industrial capacity to absorb a larger labour
force but in which existing facilities would be placed under excessive
strain by inward migration. In both cases decisions on how far to
encourage or promote migration must turn on a proper assessment
of the ability to meet social needs in the recipient areas, rather than
on a priori judgements for or against migration as such. Where
migration is necessary, both planning and manpower policies are
required to work in conjunction with each other if people are to be
located where the opportunities for employment are, or can be provided.

Manpower Policies in General

Most OECD countries have, in recent years, given increased
attention to the role that manpower policies of all kinds can play in
regional development policies, and this is to be welcomed. It would
be true of many, however, to say that they play a relatively minor role
compared with industrial incentives, infrastructure development and
physical planning. There would seem to be a strong case for reassessing
and strengthening them as part of the process of making regional
policies more effective.

Firstly, the problem of regional imbalances and disparities, in
employment, incomes and standards of living, is not to be defined only
in terms of statistical abstractions. It is in part a qualitative one,

112

of adapting people themselves to the challenges of modern society and of overcoming the disabilities, in education, knowledge and skills which have been inherited from the past. Suitable manpower policies, in the broadest sense, must therefore go hand in hand with the restructuring and the regional distribution and redistribution of economic life.

Secondly, the persistent and intractable nature of many regional problems suggests that only those policies will work effectively that pay sufficient regard to the most "intractable problem" of all, the human being himself, the variety of his needs and aspirations and responses that he will make to new situations.

Thirdly, no regional policies can (or, perhaps, should) obviate the need for movement of people, from areas of less to areas of greater opportunity. To the extent that movement is necessary, either because regional policies are inadequate to guarantee that the needs of people can be met, where they happen to be at one point of time, or because they aim at encouraging a new geographical pattern of development, measures become necessary to facilitate it.

These considerations apply most obviously in countries such as Spain, France, Japan and Australia, in which it is a specific objective of regional policy to bring about national development in accordance with a national strategy, by selective development of different growth centres, or in the United States where migration is regarded as a mainspring of national development. It applies also in countries with the opposite philosophy, of diminishing the need for migration from "problem" regions, such as the United Kingdom and Italy. In neither case can migration be altogether avoided, but whether people remain where they are, or are enabled to take advantage of better opportunities in their own regions or elsewhere, will depend on the adequacy of manpower policies, in conjunction with planning policies.

Manpower policies clearly call for action at both regional and national levels. People in "problem" regions need to be informed of and trained for opportunities elsewhere in the country as well as in their own regions. Zones for development must make allowance for inward migration from outside as well as from their own regions, if they are to contribute not only to local needs but to most of the depressed or declining regions elsewhere. Schemes for alleviating the costs of removal and resettlement should be framed with a view to facilitating movement to all the areas, zones or centres, which are capable of absorbing people from other regions. In planning development of selected growth centres the assumptions made about the source of the incoming population will themselves be a factor in determining the measures needed to enable it to come.

It would seem to be a distinct possibility that, in some countries, insufficient attention to the manpower implication of growth, and of the measures needed to facilitate migration interregionally as well as within regions have prevented other development policies having their full effect. For example, the slow growth of some new towns, maritime industrial areas, etc. , has in part been due to lack of manpower, despite the "surplus" in other parts of the country. Perhaps more importantly, the problem which has been referred to earlier, that in times of upswing, labour shortages develop while there are still large reserves of unused manpower elsewhere, has not so far been substantially lessened by regional policies. If this problem is not to remain a recurring feature, as it has in several countries throughout the history of regional policy, more weight may have to be given to the measures of manpower policy which facilitate the transfer of labour from regions in which it cannot be employed to those where it can be, under conditions which reduce the social disadvantages which unassisted and unplanned voluntary migration has occasioned.

In short, regional policies themselves need to be defined in terms of their implications for the regional distribution of manpower. Measures in the fields of education, training and relocation are in any case necessary to enable people to adjust satisfactorily to the change. If fully utilized they should enable a practical balance to be struck between alternative regional policies, in which migration or movement play a greater or lesser part, enabling movement to take place when it is necessary or desirable for national development or helping to avoid it when it is not. The limited success that has so far attended the use of other methods suggests the need for increased effort to evaluate the role of manpower measures in regional policies.

VII

QUESTIONS RELATING TO PUBLIC
FINANCE, PLANNING, CO-ORDINATION
AND ADMINISTRATION

Policies and measures use resources, human and physical, intelligence and skills, land, industrial, commercial and social equipment and buildings, materials, energy, water, communications of all sorts, hospitals, schools, colleges and universities. Marshalling resources, and steering their use in the directions required by public policy, involve measures of public finance, of planning and programming, and of administration. Theoretical objectives, general strategies and specific methods or measures, such as have been discussed in the earlier chapters of this report, are therefore, only real to the extent that they are supported by measures in these fields. They are considered in this separate chapter because they provide a common background to the policies, objectives and strategies and more specific measures which have been discussed earlier.

Public Finance

The adoption of regional policies in any country poses a number of primary questions in the field of public finance, viz:

a) How much public finance should be provided for regional policy purposes?

b) What priorities should be given, in allocating public finance, to the various purposes and measures of regional policy?

c) What institutions, organisations and bodies should have the responsibility for the spending of the finance?

d) What procedures will ensure the best use of such finance as can be provided?

These are, admittedly, theoretical questions. In practice they are rarely posed still less answered in the majority of OECD countries. The experimental and pragmatic nature of most regional policies itself involves 'ad hoc' responses to new problems and situations and additional forms and quantities of public finance. They will need, however, to be increasingly posed and answered as the aims of regional policies become more ambitious and more a permanent feature of national policies as a whole, and if the policies themselves are to be properly evaluated in terms of cost/effectiveness. The history of those countries which have already pursued regional policies over a long period of time and have devoted substantial resources of public finance to them, without altogether satisfactory results, suggests that more effective policies will require a reappraisal of the role of public finance, in terms such as those listed above.

The answer to such questions will not be uniform since countries differ so much in the need for and aims of regional policies, in their financial organisation, the role of central and local budgets and in their institutions. A report such as this can only point to the general considerations which the experience of OECD countries suggests are likely to be relevant to the answers, despite differences in particular circumstances.

It would be beguilingly simple to answer the first question, in all countries, by a single word or expression meaning "more". In all the countries that have been studied there is probably no exception to the rule that the objectives of regional policy could be more rapidly achieved if greater financial resources could be made available. This is of no help, however, for it is true of all other objectives which are claimants on national resources. Important though regional objectives are, in all countries, the Working Party can see no justification for exempting them from the tests that must be applied to all forms of public expenditure, namely, the relative urgency of the need, and what results can be achieved by the expenditure.

Even if these tests are applied, the questions would still remain: "more than what"?, "by how much more"? and "in which directions"?. They can be answered by arbitrary chosen formulae, such as X% more in general and Y% or Z% more in particular directions, but arbitrary formulae do not guarantee that the increases will be sufficient for their purposes, or will represent the best use of scarce resources. They may also cause the case for a reduction of expenditure in some directions to be overlooked. The formula that expenditure on regional policies should represent a minimum proportion of national income, or the national budget, would still be arbitrary unless the proportions were calculated by reference to the need for and effectiveness of the ways in which it was spent. "More" public finance should be

116

applied to regional policies only when the existing levels are insufficient for their purposes and when the presumrd net advantage to the community is greater than can be gained by the expenditure of the same resources in other ways.

As a specialist group, the Working Party is probably the most conscious, of all the organs of OECD, of the need for increasing the contribution that regional policies can make to the growth and progress of the Member countries. The studies they have made do not suggest that, in any country, the limit has as yet been reached beyond which further increases in public expenditure on regional policies could not be justified by their results. The impression they have formed is the contrary, that regional policies do not as yet receive sufficient priority in the allocation of public finance and that there would be justification for devoting a greater proportion of public expenditure to them.

This is an impression rather than a statement of fact and one that is difficult to substantiate by reference to the statistics of public expenditure. This is a difficulty especially peculiar to regional policy, in that, unlike expenditures on particular purposes, such as agriculture, health, education, transport and so on, regional policy expenditure does not normally come under a single head in "functional" or departmental budgets and in no country is there as yet even a "notional" budget which brings together all those elements of public expenditure which are regional in intent.

In some countries, of which France and Italy are examples, special funds have been created to supplement the ordinary departmental budgets to permit additional priority to be given to specific projects of importance for regional policy: in Canada the Department of Regional Expansion has a budget of its own: in Italy there is also a requirement, embodied in legislation, that 60% of public investment funds and 80% of new investments of all departments or ministries should be devoted to the Mezzogiorno. In many countries public expenditure by Departments and specialized Agencies incorporates expenditures for regional objectives, in communications, housing, urban development and industrial expansion or in grants, loans and subsidies to other authorities, often in such a way that it is impracticable to distinguish expenditure on regional policies from that on more general purposes.

Neither where there are special funds and policies, nor where regional expenditure is sub-sumed within Departmental expenditure is it possible to assess the real contribution that public finance makes to regional policies. Nor is one method necessarily better than the other. Special funds may be in substitution of "normal" departmental expenditure and to this extent, do not necessarily increase the total devoted to regional purposes. By the latter method regional purposes can be given more or less weight within Departmental budgets, according to policy. The former may have the advantage of centralizing the initiative and drive given to regional policies when backed up by resources, but the advantage is nullified if the resources are insufficient or obtained at the expense of diminished regional expenditure from 'normal' funds. The latter may have the disadvantage that within a Department, regional aims may be sub-ordinated to other Departmental purposes, but this disadvantage may be overcome by the decisions on priorities.

Public finance is not a matter of expenditure only, but also of revenue. The ways in which revenues can be raised by taxation, fees and charges and the scale on which they can be raised, will affect the answer to the primary questions listed at the beginning of this section. The effectiveness of regional policy, for example, may be increased by providing more finance for incentives to produce, or enhanced spending on infrastructure, but the benefit they may bring may be offset by higher taxation which diminishes the funds available to producers or those responsible for infrastructure and may lessen demand.

The choice of institutions to carry out regional policies has a bearing on both aspects of public finance, expenditure and revenue. The allocation of funds by central Government to other institutions and organisations will not effectively ensure the objectives of regional policy unless they are able and willing to use them efficiently for the specified purposes. Attention to the restructuring and reorganisation of institutions and their capacity to raise revenues is also necessary to find the right balance between central Government and other sources of public finance that can be effectively applied to regional problems.

The proposition that has been put forward earlier that there is a case for increasing the scale of public finance devoted to regional policies must be severly qualified by the principle that regional policies should not be exempted from the tests that are applied to public finance generally. There are two sides to public accounts, revenue as well as expenditure, and the effectiveness and benefits of public finance policies cannot be properly evaluated only in terms of the latter. This can affect the total amount and priorities of public expenditure and the choice of the institutions by which it is carried out.

To form a judgement of the effect that public finance policies have on regional development and of the desirability of increasing expenditure, it is clearly necessary to go behind the crude figures of actual expenditure, and to establish what they mean in real terms and in

118

terms of relative importance. Allowance must be made not only for
the changing value of money - normally falling owing to inflation - but
of the influence that public expenditure in other directions will have on
regional problems. Thus figures may show a rise in (real) expenditure
on, say, roads under a 'special' regional programme in certain
regions. It is not a true rise if the 'special' programme represents
but a substitution or diminution of "normal" expenditure and will have
an insignificant effect on regional development if it constitutes but a
small proportion of total expenditure on roads. Similarly, the
allocation of a fixed percentage of public investment to certain regions
is of no particular significance unless the percentage is different from
what it would have been under 'normal' policies. Its effects, beneficial
or otherwise, must depend on the nature and usefulness of the investment projects themselves.

In most countries public expenditure for specific regional policy
purposes appears to have risen, in absolute terms, in the five years to
1972. Available data, which is not in all cases comparable from one
country to another mainly because of the paucity of data on expenditure
on infrastructure for regional purposes, is shown below.

(In million US $ at current
prices and current exchange rates)

Belgium	Annual average	
	1962/66	17.5
	1967/70	92.4
	1971/73	118.2
Canada	1969/70	203.4
	1974/75	474.5
	(estimates)	
Finland	1971	10.1
	1974	40.8
France	Annual average	
	1961/63	40.4
	1970/72	207.0
Germany	Annual average	
	1961/63	29.5
	1967/70	54.7
	1972/74	372.4

Italy	Annual average	
	1965/70	745.6
	1971/75	2,448.0
Netherlands	Annual average	
	1967/71	38.6
	1972	77.1
Norway	1962	11.0
	1967	31.0
	1972	103.1
	(1962 at 1972 prices*)	(15.9)
	(1967 at 1972 prices*)	(40.0)
Sweden	1967/68	43.8
	1972/73	111.7
	(1967/68 at 1972 prices)	(59.0)
United Kingdom	1967/68	326.9
	1971/72	579.4
	(1971/72 at 1967/68 prices**)	(429.6)

*   At 1972 exchange rates.
** At 1968 exchange rates.

Note: The expenditure data comprise the following elements:

Canada: Expenditures of the Department of Regional Economic Expansion comprising development planning and administration, industrial incentives, infrastructure assistance, social and rural development programmes.

Finland: Interest subsidies (1971 and 1974), regional development fund (1971 and 1974), compensation for the employment of inexperienced labour (1974), industrial estates (1974), transport subsidies (1974).

France: Industry and tertiary sector: Treasury grants, FDES loans, assistance for vocational training and for mobility (inexistent in 1961/63) and public investments: FIAT (set up in 1963), Special Fund for the Renovation of Rural Areas (set up in 1967), credits for the tourism development area offices (set up in 1963, 66 and 67).

120

Germany:	Budget data in the Federal Budget, short-falls in tax revenues arising from the tax exempt investment grants instituted in 1969, funds of the "Joint Task" (Federal and Laender budgets) set up in 1972, and a few special aids of minor importance in the zonal border areas.
Italy:	1965/70: Provision under Law No. 717 of 1965 (2,800 billion lire for the 6 year period 1965/70 for the Cassa per il Mezzogiorno). 1971/75: Provision under Law No. 853 of 1971 (7,200 billion lire for the 5 years 1971/75, of which 3,125 billion directly allocated by the Law and 1,450 billion as the Cassa's potential commitment over the same period for interventions of its pertinence as well as 2,550 billion for the interest maturing on loans to industry in the period 1975/85).
Netherlands:	Regional industrialization incentives, programmes for infrastructure improvements, special regional welfare subsidies and special benefits for development centres from the Municipality Fund.
Norway:	Investments grants (1972), relocation grants (1967 and 1972), manpower training grants (1967 and 1972), settling-in grants (1967 and 1972), transport compensation grants (1972), loans and loan guarantees by the RDF.
Sweden:	Location grants, transport subsidies (1972/73), training grants (1972/73), employment grants (1972/73), loans and credit guarantees.
United Kingdom:	Expenditures on regional incentives of direct benefit to individual enterprises by the United Kingdom Government, net of loan repayments and factory rents and sales.

It cannot be established from such a broad statement that the countries have at the same time increased the priority given to regional objectives in their public finance policies. Overall public expenditure has also risen as have the needs for it, with growing populations and higher total national outputs. None of the Governments publish regular surveys which show, comprehensively, how much is being provided, year by year, in total or for separate, specific regional purposes, and whether they represent a rise in real terms, after allowing for cost changes, or in proportion to total public expenditure. The lack of such surveys also means that it is difficult to ascertain how far the emphasis of regional policy is changing, for example, as between industrial incentives, the various types of infrastructure and manpower policies generally. The fact that, in many, if not in most countries, central budgets do not have a regional element, or that, where there is a regional element, it relates only to the special regional funds rather than the totality of regional expenditure, means that too little is known about the effects, at regional level, of national budgets. So long as this state of affairs continues, assessment of the effects of public finance policies on regional development and "balance" must remain largely a matter of inference and speculation. A further disadvantage is that there is no firm basis from which to judge the scope and need for shifts between one type of regional expenditure and another.

Budgetary policies are closely linked to the organisation and structure of Government itself. The national financial "cake" must be divided between Departments or agencies as they exist. Unless and until the organisation of Government is itself regionalized (for which there are arguments on both sides) it would be academic to suggest that the difficulties referred to in the previous paragraph could be overcome by the reorganisation of central budgets, or the creation of special regional budgets incorporating all expenditures on regional policies.

Nonetheless it would seem desirable to improve methods for applying public finance to regional policy, in order to ensure that it receives its due weight in national policy and that, within the total that can be provided, funds are spent in those directions which yield the best results.

There are at least two lines of approach to this problem which would seem to deserve consideration by Governments. One is to make more use, in relation to regional policy, of PPBS (planned programmed budgetary systems). Many governments are increasingly adopting PPBS as a means of evaluating the competing claims on their budgets of different elements of expenditure, for adjusting total expenditure over a period to total revenues, and for apportioning it according to priorities. If, within each head or group of expenditures coming with the PPBS system, those elements were identified which reflected a specific regional policy purpose some progress could be made in considering the public finance implications of regional policy as a whole.

It could also lead to an advance in the second direction, towards the creation of at least a "notional" budget which would bring together all the elements in the expenditure side of the regional policy account.

Such "notional" budgets would enable both Governments and the public to be fully aware of the total scale, in terms of public finance, of their regional policy efforts and assist them in the always difficult task of deciding how far that scale, and the scale of individual items, should be modified in the light of their potential contribution to the aims of regional policy as a whole. This suggestion is put forward, not as a criticism of present policies, but because of the general need, as the Working Party believes, to give greater weight to regional policies and to public expenditure on them. To respond to that need without a full evaluation of existing expenditure, such as could be made with the help of PPBS and notional budgets, would not necessarily produce the right answers to the primary questions posed at the beginning of this section. The need also to assess the "impact" of regional policies on the problems with which they are intended to deal (see Chapter III) reinforces the case for a comprehensive examination of the role of public finance itself within the framework of normal budgetary systems.

A full picture of the public finance aspects of regional policies would, of course, not be obtainable without reference to the revenue side of the notional regional budget. This would show the sources from which the expenditure is financed, central Government, local authorities and agencies of various kinds, and how far each was contributing. It would also show how far any net increase in revenues would be necessary to match planned increases in expenditure and enable consideration to be given to the contribution that each source could make. Finally any net increases in revenue could be measured against the net income in national revenues from different sources, enabling a judgement to be made on the "share" of national revenues going to regional purposes. For example it would be possible to compare the contribution of the central budget to regional incentives for industry with the additional revenues obtained by taxation on industry, a fact that might have a significant bearing on the possibilities of further increases in the former.

The conclusion of this section can only be a general one, namely that public finance is the means by which policies find expression in a common denominator. By careful appraisal of both sides of the account its actual role and its potential for the future, can be better evaluated. Without such an appraisal, regional policies can be no more than a series of 'ad hoc' measures the impact of which would be difficult to assess, and the prospect of making them more effective correspondingly lessened. The studies of the Working Party suggest there is ample room, and need, for improving the techniques used in most countries for applying public finance to regional problems.

Planned Development and Coordination

The tasks confronting Governments which adopt regional policies divide broadly into four categories: surveying and defining the problems; formulating a general strategy; translating a general strategy into specific objectives; and, finally, devising and applying those methods and measures which will enable the objectives to be attained over a given period. To this list should be added the assessment of the results of the strategies and methods adopted, by adequate monitoring and review procedures.

Government activity alone, however, can not ensure the effective working of regional policies. It is in the response that will be made to Government policies and measures by people, industry and institutions that provides the ultimate test of the effectiveness of policies. If people continue to migrate to areas and cities in a way which does not conform to planning and settlement policies, if industry does not expand in the regions in response to incentives and investment in infrastructure, or if social facilities and institutions fail to keep pace with the need for them, the regional policies and measures can only be deemed to be ineffective and insufficient, or directed towards unattainable targets, and therefore overambitious in relation to the resources which can be made available.

The measures of the kinds previously discussed can have their desired effect only if they are attuned and applied suitably to the specific conditions of the regions in which they operate. These determine what response will be made to the individual measures, and to all the measures acting in conjunction with each other. In more concrete terms, incentives to manufacturing industry will promote such industry only when the necessary conditions, of infrastructure, housing and social services, manpower, linkages with supplies and markets, etc. , exist, or will be brought about by other policy measures. They will also only have their desired effect, on employment and incomes, if they are so designed as to stimulate those particular manufacturing industries which are capable of expanding on a sufficient scale, or of generating, through the multiplier effect, other industries and occupations which will contribute to the same aims. On the other hand, if the conditions in a region are better suited to other industries than manufacturing, for example primary industries and tourism, the use of incentives limited to manufacturing may not only promote, in so far as they are effective, the wrong kind of industry but lead to a neglect of those types of development for which the region is, in fact better suited.

The method by which specific measures, such as those previously discussed, can be attuned to circumstances of particular regions is, broadly, the preparation of general "strategies" for each region. The need for these has been indicated in Chapter V, which also outlines the broad content of strategies and the matters which have to be considered in framing an appropriate policy for regions. Some further observations are made here relating to the conditions for making effective use of general strategies.

It should be noted that most of the countries studied by the Working Party appear to recognize that the preparation of strategies for each region (and not only of "problem" regions) is essential to the successful implementation of their overall regional policies. In France, the policy of "Aménagement du Territoire", in Germany the combination of economic with spatial policies (Raumordnungspolitik), in Spain the plans for areas and zones of development, in the United Kingdom regional strategies and local structure plans, in Sweden the nationwide plan for the development of the regional structure, in the United States the "overall development plans" (ODP) required from local authorities in receipt of special regional aid, in Italy and Japan the development plans of regional authorities are only a few examples of the almost universal practice of developing a strategic framework for each region, within which measures of incentives, infrastructure development or other measures are to operate.

Judgement as to their effectiveness must however be reserved, for they are still a latter day phenomena, resulting from comparatively recent realization, in most countries, that the aims of regional policy are so wide ranging that they require the comprehensive approach that is contained in the concept of general strategies.

The studies of the Working Party suggest that there are a number of points to which attention should be given if regional strategies are to serve a useful purpose.

Firstly, they are long term in their working. Planning and construction periods are themselves lengthy, and completed projects take time before they can have their full effects. This is the more important the larger the scale of changes in a region's economic and social structure that are necessary, the greater the expansion of industry or the more comprehensive the necessary development of physical infrastructure.

A long time scale means also that a strategy can only be progressively implemented, each successive phase depending on the accomplishments of preceding phases. Flexibility is essential, both to adjust longer term aims in the light of the implementation of the earlier phases and to take account of change in the underlying problems, as economic and social conditions, and techniques and technologies themselves change. Monitoring, review and continued "roll forward" in time are essential both to the progressive implementation of a strategy and to flexibility in adapting the strategy to changing circumstances.

Secondly, a strategy becomes a purely paper exercise unless its objectives are realistic. "Realism" is a word with harsh connotations. It is often used in opposition to the idealism which does not fear to set objectives which are beyond reach. Even unattainable goals have the merit of encouraging positive and constructive action, based on the conviction that some progress towards them is better than none at all and that, in time, they will come nearer to attainment. On this view "realism" serves only to hamper, discourage and restrain necessary action and leads to a defeatist acceptance of goals which fall short of what is attainable and desirable. Our use of the term "realism" is not intended to justify such attitudes or to decry the usefulness of working towards goals which may not be fully attainable. We argue only that a realistic rather than a wishful thinking view of what given strategies and methods of regional policy can be expected to achieve over a period is desirable, if the best and most effective use of the resources they require is to be made.

From this point of view the experience of OECD countries which have attempted to formulate regional strategies suggests that there are three main elements in a realistic approach to them:

a) They should be consistent with the scale of resources that is likely to be available for them.

b) There should be consistency between the objectives of national and regional strategies.

c) The specific objectives within a region should be those which are calculated to promote regional development in ways which will best resolve the particular problems with which the region is faced.

These may seem to be self-evident propositions but they are worth asserting, since their observance should prove of practical use to countries whose regional strategies are in need of revision, or are in an early stage of formulating them. As has been noted more than once in this report, the record of regional policies over the years has not been one of unequivocal success. This is obviously not attributable to any one cause but the Working Party does not hesitate to suggest that observance of these principles should help to make regional policies more effective in the future.

With regard to a) it should be noted that the total resources likely to be available is the sum of what will be generated from within a region itself, as it progresses in economic development and as its own resources are better mobilized for regional purposes, and of the transfers to the region from outside. These latter resources are not only the direct transfers from central budgets to finance incentives or to promote infrastructure development but also include the capital investment, of the public and private sectors, in directions and to the extent that such investment can be attracted. As has been noted elsewhere there are limiting factors in both respects. The numerous claims on central budgets for all purposes usually exceed the resources than can be provided without creating inflationary pressures. Other priorities besides those of regional "balance" preclude unlimited transfer to regional objectives. A regional strategy will therefore not be realistic if it is based on too optimistic a view of what can be transferred from central sources for its purposes. One implication of this is that a strategy for a particular region is more likely to be realistic if it is the outcome of a joint assessment of the available resources by those who prepare the strategy and those who will bear the main costs, whether they are wholly within central Government itself or partly in central Government and partly in the regions. Experience in the United Kingdom, for example, has shown that the earlier regional strategies prepared by the regional economic planning councils were not in all respects adequate as guides to future regional development, partly because they tended for the most part to concentrate more on a valuable diagnosis of regional problems than on a specific regional strategy for programmed action within the overall limits of national resource restraints. The conclusion drawn from this experience was that regional strategies should in future be prepared by a joint organisation in which central and local Government as well as the planning Councils co-operated. It is hoped thereby to achieve greater realism all round.

Realism is also necessary in the second respect. Over-optimistic estimates of the amount of additional or mobile industry that can be attracted by incentives and infrastructure development can lead to an unviable strategy and to "frustrated" expenditure in the sense that it does not produce its intended results, e.g. that roads actually built carry little traffic and become empty monuments to a grand but unrealistic design.

Emphasis must also be laid on b) since if regional and national strategies (where they exist) pursue conflicting objectives they will tend to nullify rather than complement each other. Thus a national strategy which seeks to promote rapid economic development or a high growth rate, may demand a concentration of resources in those regions which are most capable of such development and growth. If, however, the strategies for each individual region reflect a policy of directing resources in ways which will rectify interregional imbalances at the expense of national growth, they will be in conflict with national strategy. Each regional strategy will only be realistic if it takes account of the way such conflict is to be resolved. This applies to "problem" and other regions alike. In more concrete terms, strategies for heavily industrialized or "prosperous" regions, such as the South East or West Midlands regions in the United Kingdom, or the Northern regions in Italy, must be conditioned by the national strategies which seek to restrain their development in order to give preference to the "problem" regions of Scotland, Northern England or Southern Italy, and use means such as licensing and investment preferences on a large enough scale to implement such a policy. By contrast a strategy in a backward or declining region which presupposes that they will receive a greater preference in national policies than is in fact the case will be equally unrealistic.

We have referred earlier to the fact that strategies for individual regions cannot be realistic if, in sum, they presuppose greater population and economic growth than the nation as a whole is capable of. They will also be unrealistic if a series of policies, national and regional, are pursued without sufficient recognition of their interaction. The fact that many countries have made more progress in preparing strategies for individual regions than in national strategies for regional development, which show clearly how the individual strategies are related to each other, suggests that there may well be too high an element of unreality in some of the strategies for individual regions, more especially in those countries which do not attempt to provide a comprehensive national framework, even in the most indicative form, for the regional strategies. Countries with formal national strategies with a regional "component" include Sweden, Spain, Italy and France. Perhaps France has gone further with the drawing up every five years of a national plan in which the forecasts for employment and for infrastructure investments are regionalized with a high degree of detail.

The third point c) will be equally self-evident but its importance should not be underestimated. The use of nationally administered instruments of regional policy, incentives, restraints, infrastructure investment, etc. , can only be effective if they are applied in each region in accordance with the specific characteristics of its problems and its scope for development in ways which will resolve those problems. Regions differ considerably in their economic and social structure and the response they can make to the various measures designed to promote their progress. The policy instruments or methods will therefore work differently in each region and call, accordingly, for a different strategy.

This principle appears to be more widely recognized and accepted now than in earlier post war decades when regional policies tended to concentrate on the provision of forms of external assistance to problem regions, with less attention paid to the origins and causes of the problems or to the kind of local response which the assistance could generate. Both the relative failure of earlier measures to have the necessary impact on the local regional situation, as, for example, in Italy and the United Kingdom, and the widening of the scope of regional policies to include planned development on a national scale have focussed increasing attention on the importance of correctly appraising the local conditions, within each region, which are specific to it, and devising strategies which fit those conditions.

The questions which arise in devising strategies suited to local conditions are of course numerous. Is development to be concentrated in large urban centres or to be dispersed in a balanced manner over the whole region? Is the decline in agricultural employment to be offset by local manufacturing, service industries or by rural housing of commuters to well located larger centres? Should economic development be primarily directed to export to other regions or to the local market? Will small scale industry better serve the unemployment problem than large scale? In what way can aptitudes and skills be better developed, and for what kind of employment? Should reliance be placed on the introduction of externally based industry or the development and expansion of local enterprise? Is the necessary growth in industry best obtained from industries involving advanced technology or will progress be best achieved, and be more long lasting, if it is focussed on the step-by-step process known as intermediate technology? What kind of infrastructure development is required for each of those alternatives, and in what order should roads, ports, schools, hospitals, housing, water supplies and sewage and effluent disposal projects be provided? What restraints on land utilization are necessary for planned location of industry, housing and amenities? Is there likely to be enough local knowledge and initiative, and an adequate organisation to utilize the assistance that can be externally provided or can effective steps be taken to encourage it in order to diminish the risk of permanent dependence on external sources of development? Is foreign assistance likely to be needed and acceptable, and in what respects should local development be modified to suit the requirements of foreign investors? Finally, what impact on the basic problems, of employment or unemployment, low incomes and unsatisfactory environment, or of congestion, overheating or need for planned settlement will the alternative policies have?

Questions such as these cannot be answered theoretically but through detailed investigation, survey and evaluation of local conditions in the regions. The test of the realism of a strategy, however, lies not in the clarity with which its objectives are defined but in the evidence that sufficient study has been made of local conditions to permit reasoned answers to such questions.

Organisational and Institutional Change

Regional policies pose the question of what forms of organisation, within Governments and in relation to the institutions concerned, will best enable them to be implemented. As in other issues of methodology each country must seek a solution suited to its own special circumstances but it is possible to point to a number of considerations which general experience suggests need to be taken into account.

Foremost of these is, perhaps, that most of the countries that have been studied by the Working Party have found it necessary to adapt their administrative machinery to the special requirements of regional policies. The main reason for this is that regional policies, their objectives and methods, cut across the normal boundaries of Government Departments, local authorities and public institutions. They impinge on most aspects of economic and social policy and require action from a multiplicity of bodies each of which has responsibility and power of action in its own particular field.

Two special problems arise directly from this. First, where should the primary responsibility lie for ensuring that regional policies secure their proper place among the competing, rival claims which require the attention of the Government as a whole? Secondly, how should the efforts of the Ministries' organisations and institutions which are concerned with particular aspects of regional policies be coordinated, to ensure harmonization of objectives and action to implement them? There is a third issue also, which is how to assign, among all the bodies that can play a part in regional policy, responsibility for individual aspects and tasks? The Working Party is convinced from its studies that the ultimate efficacy of regional policy, and its ability to make a significant impact on the problems with which it is supposed to deal, will turn to a large extent on how well the administrative machinery is designed for these tasks.

There are many different ways in which individual countries administer their regional policies. In part the differences reflect the constitutional structure, the number and size of Government Departments, the organisation of the executive branch of Government as a whole and its relation to the legislature. In unitary states they reflect also the system of local Government, the functions and size of the units and their relations to central Government. In Federal States they reflect in addition the division of powers between the Federal and component States and, within them, those of the more local authorities.

This partly, but not wholly, accounts for some of the differences in approach to the problems of organisation for regional policies. Some are also due to the differing nature and weight of the regional policy objectives - the overcoming of economic disparities in some or the promotion of planned spatial development in others. These are, undoubtedly, due also to the fact that some countries have given more deliberate attention to the special problems of organisation than others. Even those that have done so, however, have reached varied conclusions and no clear pattern, either of practice or principle, is discernible.

There clearly can be no single 'ideal' solution to the problems of administration. The test by which any system of organisation must be judged is whether it makes adequate provision for the specific tasks to be accomplished. The tasks of regional policy as they have been described in this report, are inherently of a managerial kind. They involve the gathering and assessment of facts (intelligence); defining aims; devising policies and methods; implementing them; coordination and supervision; and monitoring and reviewing. Each of these breaks down into sub-tasks.

The Working Party are of one mind in believing that regional policies should be a permanent, continuing feature of national policies, with essentially long term aims. On this basis, a systematic evaluation of the tasks which they entail, and the organisation which they would require would be amply justified. Such an evaluation may well lead to the conclusions that at least the main "strategic" issues, of intelligence, aims and principles of policy, coordination, monitoring and review should be dealt with, under the collective guidance of the Government, by a single Department of State rather than diffused among many, with the task of execution and operation of measures being carried out by those central Departments, regional and local authorities and organisations which have the requisite special expertise or local knowledge.

VIII

INTERNATIONAL ASPECTS

As indicated in the Introduction, regional policies have an impact
beyond national frontiers and also offer a field for co-operative
endeavour amongst nations pledged, as in the OECD to pursue mutually
beneficial policies. In the pre-war and earlier post-war periods
regional policies tended to be regarded as entirely a matter of
domestic concern, involving primarily an effort to promote development in selected areas. Neither the scale on which they were pursued,
nor the methods adopted appeared to give rise to problems of an
international character. In the Working Party's view the time has,
however, now come to recognize that there are certain aspects of
regional policies which cannot be considered in a limited national context
but require both thought and action on the international plane.

In the last few years there have been many signs that this principle
is finding acceptance in the international community, particularly in
Europe. Thus the OECD itself has been responsible, through the
Working Party, for a continuous exchange of information on all aspects
of regional policy and in its reports* has demonstrated the necessity
for co-operation. In the wider context of international investments,
especially those connected with international trade and economic development, OECD is seeking to achieve strengthened co-operation
amongst its Member countries. The impact of internal policies,
including regional policy, on international trade, is an important
aspect of this work. The Council of Europe has directed considerable
effort through conferences at Ministerial**, regional and municipal***

---

*   "The Regional Factor in Economic Development", OECD, 1970. "Issues of
Regional Policy", OECD, 1973.

**   European Conference of Ministers Responsible for Regional Planning.
***   European Conference of Local Authorities.

level, to promote co-operation on regional planning between their Member countries. In the EEC there is now explicit recognition, embodied in the proposal to establish a European regional development fund, that the regional problems of individual countries are of concern to the Community as a whole. In addition it is recognized that agricultural, social and manpower policies need to be structured so as to take account also of regional policies.

Since the OECD includes countries outside both European organisations it is appropriate to recognize that the need for understanding of, and co-operation on, the international aspects of regional policies cannot be confined to the countries which are members of these two organisations. This understanding is necessary, both because of the importance of regional development in most countries and for the repercussions that regional policies have in the international sphere. There is a mutual interest in the success of regional policies and a need to harmonize them so that they serve the general objectives of economic and social progress in the international community at large.

It seems to us that certain action designed to institute co-operation that would be of advantage to all those involved could be undertaken on at least three fronts: firstly, as regards frontier regions, including peripheral maritime regions; secondly, with regard to rules for the granting of incentives to ensure harmonization of conditions concerning location of enterprises and the utilization of available manpower; thirdly, study of the consequences for regional policy, especially for large regions marked by structural stagnation, of changes in the international economy.

It is not part of the purpose of this report to examine in detail the specific issues which arise between individual countries. The Working Party is aware of the work being done by the Council of Europe to promote co-operation amongst its Member countries as regards mountain regions, border areas, frontier regions and especially the maritime regions in the periphery of Europe and considers that efforts to secure and strengthen international co-operation in these fields deserve the fullest support by the Government concerned.

As has been noted in Chapter VI, incentives form a necessary, indeed essential, part of regional policies. They are designed to encourage the establishment of industries, and increasingly tertiary sector activities, in backward or declining regions in accordance with general regional strategies. The precise nature and forms of incentives reflect the domestic problems of the countries concerned and they do not, as such, give rise to questions of an international character. Interventions which are domestically oriented but which may have incidental trade effects are not necessarily incompatible with international conventions such as those of GATT or the OECD itself. Though industrial incentives for purposes of regional policy have a comparatively recent history this fact alone would not justify singling them out as requiring special consideration in the context of international relations.

Nonetheless the use of incentives for regional policies has certain aspects which appear to deserve study in the international context. It is clear to the Working Party that incentives form a necessary, and essential, part of regional policies of most countries, and indeed have tended to increase in scale and importance. In an organisation such as OECD which by its Convention, is pledged "to contribute to the expansion of world trade on a multilateral non-discriminatory basis in accordance with international obligations" it is legitimate to pose the question whether the widespread use of regional incentives is open to any objection from this point of view. It has been noted by the Working Party in this connection that the Report of the High Level Group on Trade and Related Problems to the Secretary-General of OECD* draws attention to the need to strengthen the effort to give effect to this pledge and calls into question the widespread use of subsidies and other government interventions of various kinds, including those for regional policy purposes, which may not only distort competition but reduce the advantages that could be obtained through the working of the principle of comparative costs. The Working Party intends to review this question further in the course of its future work.

Difficulties in establishing facts and in comparing incentives granted by different countries preclude however any simple judgement on these matters. The Working Party has noted that the EEC has established certain rules, relating to subsidies in central areas within the framework of the Community's approach to regional policy. How far there could be a case for adopting some common rules relating to regional incentives in the wider organisation of the OECD, calculated to strengthen its effort to promote mutually beneficial economic policies by co-operation and to harmonize the internal and external interest of Member countries is a matter which merits further study without prejudging what the outcome would be.

The third field in which international co-operation is necessary is in assessing the influence of major changes in international economic factors on regional problems, particularly those of larger regions marked by structural stagnation and decline. It is clear that major changes in economic growth, international competitive and marketing conditions, inflation and counter-inflationary measures, wide fluctuations in exchange rates, have external repercussions and these may

*   Policy Perspectives for International Trade and Economic Relations, OECD, 1972.

135

bear particularly on problem regions in other countries. When trade and investment barriers between co-operating countries are reduced or removed or measures taken for promoting greater financial and economic union, effects can be felt not only on individual sectors but on the economy of whole regions and may bring disadvantages to regions on the periphery of the wider trading area which could accentuate those from which they may already suffer. Since regional policies seek to strengthen the economy of disadvantaged regions, often peripheral, the need for co-operation to enable them to adjust to the new situation created by the reduction of barriers and to make the progress for which regional policy is designed becomes still more significant. There is therefore scope for examining how best to minimize adverse repercussions or to enable the changes in the international economy to help rather than impede the achievement of regional policy objectives of co-operating countries.

The case for international co-operation in relation to all the matters referred to in this chapter is in the Working Party's view well established. The resolving of regional problems is a social and political necessity in most countries. For this reason the Working Party considers it necessary for the OECD to give continuing attention to the possibilities of international co-operation in the fields indicated.

136

IX

CONCLUSIONS

This report has given a broad description of the main problems which call for specifically "regional" policies and has examined the more important issues which confront Governments in devising and carrying them out. The examination has been made on the basis of studies undertaken by the Working Party so far and, inevitably, is incomplete. Some issues of considerable importance (e. g. how account should be taken of people's preferences for alternative policies, or how a greater degree of public participation in the process of policy formulation can be secured) have not as yet been sufficiently studied to permit discussion in this report. Some - such as the subject of Chapter VIII - have only been briefly touched upon to indicate the direction in which further study will be required. Because experience is continually evolving and new lessons are being learned, there is always a need for review and re-appraisal of the issues which have been dealt with. It is hoped that the report may nonetheless prove helpful to Governments and the OECD itself as they seek to tackle the problems which arise in a constantly changing world.

The aim of this Chapter is to draw together some of the more general points which have emerged from the report, rather than to recapitulate or summarize what can be found in the body of the report. These general points are those which, in the view of the Working Party, need to be kept in the forefront in any reviews of regional policies that may be made by member Governments individually or by OECD as a whole.

One. Regional policy can be regarded, within countries and internationally, as having come of age. It can no longer be regarded as a temporary and marginal element in the management of national economies. It is, so far as we can judge, here to stay. In the increasingly complex conditions of the modern world policies framed only at the global national level, or in purely local terms, cannot effectively cope with the diversity of **situations** which arise in those relatively large parts of a country which can be designated as regions. There is therefore likely to be a continuing if not permanent need for a "regional component", and a substantial one at that, in the economic and social policies of most countries. This extends beyond the problem regions to all the regions which are inter-related and inter-dependent. A country consists of its regions, a fact that calls for national and regional policies to be made consistent with each other.

Two. The history of regional policies so far is one of mixed success, and this has important implications for the future. We cannot point to any country that has been able, despite determined and considerable effort over long periods, to achieve the objectives it has set for itself. This is due both to the difficulties inherent in the objectives and to their widening and more ambitious scope. It should be also noted that it is difficult to isolate the effects of regional policies from those of other influences that are at work, and there is no precise standard by which the success or otherwise of policies can be measured. Among the countries which have been in the lead, notably the United Kingdom and Italy, though much has been achieved, the same problems exist today as existed three or four decades ago. This is not surprising since many of the problems are continually re-inforced over many decades. Thus the steady decline in the labour needs of agriculture and coal-mining have ensured that the areas affected have remained in need of attention. There is therefore no room for complacency, or belief that there is no need for any re-appraisal of the policies which have been adopted in the past. In such a situation there is clearly a need to review and re-appraise policies from time to time. The burden of this report is that regional policies are a very necessary and important element of the totality of national policies. It is desirable therefore to make use of the experience that has been gained over the years, and which is reflected in this report, so that the policies can be made as effective as possible.

Three. The "regional problem" is not a single one. Considerations of political expediency and social equity are mixed with those of economic efficiency. Social and economic imbalance between regions cannot be the sole basis of regional policy. Many imbalances or disparities are a normal and necessary feature of all economies and of a changing and progressing world. It is unrealistic to frame regional policies solely on such concepts as regional deviations from national averages or on all such deviations, since many deviations are inevitable. It would be helpful if those that are unacceptable and capable of rectification could be more precisely defined. Regional policy is also concerned with a forward looking adaptation to change, to ensure that regions contribute to national advancement in accordance with their needs and potential and to avoid the creation of new unacceptable inequities and imbalances.

There is, therefore, an element of long term strategic planning in regional policy designed to reconcile national development with the specific characteristics of the individual regions.

Four.   Regional problems will not solve themselves, or disappear as a result of regionally undifferentiated national policies of economic growth which can accentuate, as well as alleviate, unacceptable regional disparities.   At the same time, regional policies, if framed with regard to their effect on national growth, can promote growth and the process of adaptation.   If this is done regional policies offer possibilities of better utilization of the capabilities of different regions and of regulating economic growth and social change in ways which avoid adverse effects.   There is, therefore, a need to reconcile the objectives of national and regional policies so that they harmonize and do not conflict with each other.

Five.   We have noted the large size, in terms of area and population, of the regions which are treated as "problem regions" in some countries.   The larger these areas in total, the more difficult becomes the problem of allocating sufficient investment in order to secure balanced regional development and the more necessary to consider the possibility of alternatives.   There might be a possibility that overall growth could be seriously affected by policies that devote or direct a high proportion of currently available investment resources to regions which lack the necessary conditions for growth.   On the other hand, on the basis of many concrete instances, it is apparent that a more important investment effort in extensive under-developed regions could be an essential condition for general growth.   Regional policies are concerned with developing all parts of a country while directing individual measures to particular areas after careful consideration of their competing needs and capabilities.   They must take account of the importance of diversifying and widening productive structures and market possibilities to avoid the diseconomies connected with over concentration of industrial and urban developments and the individual and social costs connected with massive migratory movements.   This should be regarded as an additional reason for careful evaluation of the scale of the problems which justify regionally differentiated policies and of the merits of the alternative policies.   An effective regional policy is, of course, unlikely to be confined to one type of solution.

Six.   There would seem to be scope in most countries for improving the definition of regional objectives in order to give them greater realism and precision, with due regard of course to the fact that political values and judgements will determine the ultimate choice.   To secure such an improvement necessitates a systematic process of evaluation of alternatives in terms of resources required and likely results.

Seven. The range of regional policy objectives is wide and comprehends the improvement of living standards in all regions. They cannot therefore be confined to any one aspect of general progress but extend to economic growth, infrastructure and social development, land use and urban planning objectives. We see the best hope for the future of regional policies in a comprehensive integration of objectives through related regional and national strategies based on assessments of prospective, rather than past, changes in the underlying conditions of population growth, technology and trade relations and people's aspirations and preferences which govern what is desirable, feasible and attainable. Assessments of future prospects should be monitored and reviewed, and objectives adjusted to changes in the assumptions on which they are based.

Eight. Regional change results from the general process of change in society and the economy and the problem for policy is partly how to facilitate change which is beneficial or unavoidable, and how to resist it or mitigate its effects if these are socially (and politically) adverse. Neither an attempt to impose a strait jacket on necessary development and change (e. g. to maintain a pre-existing pattern of population), nor a passive acceptance of the disadvantages that may arise from change (such as the over concentration of population in some areas or the decline and stagnation in others) can be a satisfactory basis for policy or wholly practicable. Recognition and analysis of the nature of the major changes which are occurring and constitute the "mainsprings" of a country's general progress represents however a first and essential step in devising suitable policies, both national and regional.

Nine. Regional policies have social and political as well as economic aims but it is appropriate for a body concerned inter-alia with economic co-operation and development to stress the importance of a correct application of economic principles to regional policies. Some of the activities carried out as part of regional policies are resource users and compete with other claims on resources. Many are also means of mobilizing resources, especially latent or under-used resources such as unemployed, or under-employed labour, thereby enhancing national output. However, it cannot be assumed as an axiom that the net effect of regional policies will be of benefit to economic growth. This will depend on the nature of the policies and their effectiveness. We accept that regional policies should be subjected to the scrutiny or application of economic principles in the same way as other policies, i. e. that their net costs as well as their net benefits (in economic and social terms) should be carefully assessed. This means, as far as possible, not only assessing the direct costs and benefits but also those, respectively, saved or foregone by comparison with the alternative use of the same resources. We believe that this principle is increasingly applied in many countries. It is difficult to apply but to ignore it may lead to misuse of resources and failure rather than success in the achievement of policy objectives. Given the increasing scale on which regional policies are pursued this principle should be applied as far as it is possible to do so.

Ten. It should however be emphasized that regional policies are not conceived in terms of economic growth alone. Many countries are giving increasing attention to the regional structure in terms of the distribution of population, the pattern of urban and rural settlement, the problem of preventing excessive growth of the larger cities and the social problems resulting from internal migration, to mention only some which are social as well as economic problems. The question whether it is desirable to restrain growth in some regions and encourage it in others poses a complex range of inter-related issues which cannot be considered in terms of economic principle alone. Social as well as political considerations must therefore play a considerable part in determining the most appropriate policies.

Eleven. We have drawn attention to the need to assess adequately the scale of the problems which call for measures of regional policies and the likely impact that those measures will have. We believe that this is one of the more significant lessons of experience. We have noted that few, if any countries have so far published any evaluations of the results that their policies have or can be expected to achieve over a given time scale. We recommend that high priority be given in the future to such assessments.

Twelve. We have studied, and discussed at some length the use of financial incentives to firms, to encourage their location in preferred areas or regions. We accept that they are a key instrument for regional policies and can see no reason, in principle, to object to subsidization of enterprises for purposes of regional policies. Indeed we would go further and assert that subsidization and incentives are justifiable in economic terms to the extent that they represent an attempt to overcome the divergence between marginal private costs and marginal social costs (i. e. costs to the community at large of an individual investment) and to steer such limited mobile industry as is available to the regions most in need of it. Nonetheless we have drawn attention to some possible dangers: incentives may not always be effective, they may encourage inefficiency, promote development in ways less suited to the needs of particular regions, increase their long term dependence on such measures and reduce the possibilities of self-sustaining growth based on local as well as external enterprise, and they may result in international rivalry and overbidding. In total cost to the economy they may also be large. We believe there is a case for reviewing the systems in use so as to derive some benefit from mutual experience and minimize the dangers referred to. Further consideration of their scope as an element of regional policy would be desirable.

Thirteen. Our studies have shown that regional policies based on incentives alone cannot achieve the desired results. Attention must be given to the reasons why certain regions lag behind others, or why some are better placed than others for accommodating future growth. A wide range of other measures may be necessary, including manpower education and training, the remedying of deficiencies in social services, the improvements of local infrastructures and the planning of national infrastructures in accordance with regional needs and the fostering of "service" industries and alternatives to manufacturing activities.

Fourteen. In a few countries measures to restrain development in certain "pressure" regions complement the stimulation efforts in other regions. Experience so far does not permit a judgement on how far such measures are capable of making a major contribution to the aims of regional policies. Further study of this subject will however be undertaken by the Working Party.

Fifteen. The effectiveness of regional policies has been seen to depend, not only on the nature of the measures adopted but also on the context in which they operate. The liability of most economies to fluctuations is a factor which needs to be borne in mind, both in determining the policies required and in assessing the effect they may have. The need for flexibility in the application of policies derives from this as well as other factors, such as the discovery of new resources, the working of "voluntary" migration, the working of "self-adjusting" mechanisms and the result of the policies themselves. Monitoring of the context in which regional policies operate is a constant requirement if the policies themselves are to be relevant to the actual conditions at any point of time.

Sixteen. Most measures used for regional policies involve the use of public funds. These funds may originate from the revenues of authorities of different kinds - central, regional and local. It is difficult to assess the scale on which public finance is in fact used for regional policies. In most countries data on the contribution of authorities outside central Government is lacking while central Government statements of expenditure by individual Departments or Ministries or of central Government Agencies do not necessarily distinguish regional policy expenditure from their general expenditure which may itself contain elements of regional expenditure. We would see advantage if Governments were to attempt to identify all those expenditures of central Government and other authorities which are designed for defined regional policy purposes. If these could be brought together in the form of a single statement or "notional budget" a better appreciation could be gained of the nature and scale of the total financial effort which is being made and of its likely impact on the problems.

Seventeen. We consider that regional policies pose special problems of organisation, at both national and local levels. The reason is that regional problems cut across the normal functions or subjects of "functional" Departments of Governments, and, at the local level, local authority systems are often not geared to consider and act upon problems of a regional character. The multiplicity of objectives and the diffusion of responsibility between several authorities and agencies also gives rise to special problems, of co-ordination between them and of developing a common approach to general strategies. The need for co-ordination and a central strategy or framework of guiding principles poses the question of how best to carry out this task. Organisation is also an issue affected by the political and constitutional systems for distributing responsibilities between different bodies and for securing adequate interest and involvement or "participation" by the public as such. Clearly, countries differ too much in their political and administrative institutions for any one organisational method to be recommended as the best solution. Frequent changes have been made, in many countries, to adapt organisation to cope with the special tasks which are involved in regional development matters. We consider that the lessons of experience which have been gained should be carefully examined with particular reference to those features to which attention is drawn in this report.

Eighteen. We have drawn attention to the aspects of regional policies which are of possible international interest, particularly in the field of co-operation in regional development and incentive measures and of dealing with the effects of major economic changes on the large disadvantaged regions with which regional policies are particularly concerned. The Working Party consider that these aspects should be taken into account as countries develop their policies, and proposes also to give them further attention in its continuing work.

Nineteen. Our final point is the most general of all. Because regional problems present a continuing long term challenge of considerable magnitude they need to be tackled vigorously and regional development policy systematically integrated with the broader national economic and social policies and objectives. What this entails has been indicated in the report as a whole. The Working Party is aware of the many difficulties in the task but is convinced that the effort will be justified in the long run by its results.

Annex

CHECK-LIST OF CENTRAL GOVERNMENT INCENTIVES TO PROMOTE INDUSTRIAL LOCATION FOR REGIONAL POLICY PURPOSES

The attached check-list of central Government incentives to promote industrial location for regional policy purposes is accompanied by country notes showing in broad terms the coverage of the areas to which the incentives apply and, secondly, the main features of the incentives. The check-list and notes show the position up to March 1974.

INCENTIVES \ COUNTRY	AUSTRIA	BELGIUM	CANADA	DENMARK	FINLAND	FRA
I. Investment grants						
- on industrial building		A b)	A	A		A
- on plant and machinery			A	A		A
II. Provision of factory buildings and sites at low cost				A	A	
III. Loans						
- at market rates					A	
- at subsidized rates	A	A		A	A	A
- guaranteed	A	A	A	A	C	
IV. Fiscal concessions						
- on investment	A a)	A			A	A
- on profits					A	A
- on revenue from State aid				A		
- on State charges, local taxes, licence fees, etc.		A			A	A
V. Grants towards labour costs		—				
VI. Assistance for working costs				A c)		
VII. Labour training aids	A	A	C	A	A	A
VIII. Assistance for settling-in costs					A	
IX. Grants for moving costs					A	A
X. Financial aids to worker mobility away from designated areas	A	C			C	
XI. Financial aids to worker mobility into designated areas	A	C		A	C	A
XII. Shareholding		A			A	A
XIII. Transport and other public service concessions	A				A	A
XIV. Preferential treatment in the award of Government contracts						

Symbols: A - Available.
            B - Available but not particularly important.
            C - Available throughout the country.

NOTES:

a) Terminated at the end of 1973.
b) Interest subsidies are the normal forms of aid, but a capital bonus equivalent in value may be taken as an alternative.
c) Available to firms facing exceptional difficulty.
d) Firms may opt for this form of aid, but in such cases the amount of interest subsidy is deducted from the grant.

	GREECE	IRELAND	ITALY	JAPAN	NETHER-LANDS	NORWAY	PORTUGAL	SPAIN	SWEDEN	SWITZER-LAND	TURKEY	UNITED KINGDOM
		A	A		A	A		A	A			A
		A	A		A	A		A	A^k)			A
		A	B	A		A						A
						A						A
d)		A	A	A	B			A	A		A	A
		A			A	A			A			
e)	A	A	A	A	A	A	A	A	A	h)	A	
	A	A	A					A	A	h)	A	A
											A	A
	A^f)		A^g)						A	h)		A
												A
A	C	A	C	C	C	A	A	C	A	C^i)	C	A
			B									A
						A			A			
			B			B						A
				A		B			B			
		A			A				B			A
A^e)			B			A			A	A		
A^e)	A		A						B	A	A	

n the Eastern border areas only.
Exemption from employers' social security contributions.
Reduction of employers' social security contributions.
Various fiscal concessions are applied by the Cantonal Governments.
Applied by Cantonal Governments.
Available in exceptional circumstances.

AUSTRIA

I. COVERAGE OF THE INCENTIVES

Problem areas in which the incentives apply cover the following:

- Predominantly agricultural districts.

- Industrial areas where the main industries are faced with structural difficulties.

- Eastern border areas.

- Districts with insufficient infrastructure.

- Mining districts.

- Hill farming districts in Alpine regions.

II. MAIN FORMS OF INCENTIVES

1. Tax concessions

Accelerated depreciation for investment in movable assets (60% against 50% in the rest of the country) was allowed in certain frontier areas. (This concession was terminated in 1972 but prolonged for one year.)

2. Preferential loans

Large, medium and small-sized loans (more than AS 500,000 from AS 100,000 to AS 500,000; from AS 10,000 to AS 100,000) at 5% p. a. from 5 to 10 years according to the kind of investment are available from the Austrian Recovery Programme Fund for manufacturing and service firms. In the case of the special programme to provide

alternative employment for coal miners and to create new industrial
jobs in the eastern border areas 15 year loans are available at a 1%
p. a. rate of interest for the first 5 years and at 5% p. a. for the
remaining years, including 5 years free of redemption. Credits from
the Austria Municipal Credit Fund (Kommunalkredit-AG) are available
for factory building. A number of other specialized institutions
finance and support industrial investment, including small and medium
sized businesses and the development of tourism, although they do
not have specific regional policy aims.

3.   Employment promotion and labour mobility aids

Three types of measures are used.   i) Measures to increase
occupational and geographical mobility (training, change of domicile,
long-distance commuting).   Grants and subsidies may be given either
to companies or to workers.   ii) Measures to offset short-term
fluctuations in employment.   Subsidies are provided to support civil
engineering projects providing jobs for the unemployed or those
threatened by unemployment and also to help building construction
companies and agricultural and forestry enterprises to carry on with
their work in the winter months.   iii) Measures to safeguard jobs
in areas threatened by stagnation as a result of structural weakness.

Note

Under the Intergovernmental Fiscal Adjustment System, funds
are remitted to the provinces for regional economic promotion on the
understanding that matching contributions of one third or half are made
by the provinces.

BELGIUM

I.   COVERAGE OF THE INCENTIVES

The 1970 law on economic expansion allows 25% of the total
population of Belgium to be covered.

II.   MAIN FORMS OF INCENTIVES

1.   Tax concessions

- Real Estate Income Tax exemption during maximum 5 years,
on buildings, land and equipment.

149

- Exemption from the maximum 2% capital registration tax levied on capital contributions to the setting up of new companies or the extension of existing companies, in development areas.

- Depreciation at twice the normal annual straightline depreciation during a maximum of three assessable periods.

2. Interest subsidies

These can reach 5% over 5 years to a ceiling of 75% of the total investments and are applied to loans from approved credit institutions and for ordinary and convertible bonds under certain conditions. These 5% can be raised to 6% in the case of investments in advanced technology in the framework of a progress contract and to 7% if economic conditions make it desirable, but not such that the effective rate falls below 1%. Conditions vary according to the category of development area. Up to a maximum of 3 initial years, the interest subsidies may be allowed on the total amount of the subsidized loan.

In order not to disadvantage self-financing, a capital subsidy equivalent in value to the interest subsidy may be taken as an alternative.

3. Loan guarantees

State guarantees may be given for repayment of capital and interest; these are limited to 75% where the loan is not provided by a public credit institution.

4. Manpower training assistance

A financial intervention may be allowed in the expenses, principally remunerations and social security charges, incurred by the enterprises in the training of workers: practically between 25 and 35% for on-the-job training in Belgium, maximum 50% for the training period abroad.

5. New contractual measures

The 1970 legislation provided for a coordination of interventions on the basis of contracts with the State requiring on the part of interested enterprises an expansion of their activities in accordance with the plan's objectives.

6. Provision of factory sites

State subsidies can be allowed for setting up and equiping industrial zones.

CANADA

I. COVERAGE OF THE INCENTIVES

Under the Regional Incentives Act of 1969 (amended in 1970 and new regulations introduced in 1974), assistance is available to help in the location, expansion and modernization of manufacturing and processing activities, as well as certain types of commercial activities with a view to creating new employment in designated regions. Such regions, which are divided into three categories, contain nearly 40% of Canada's population and labour force

II. MAIN FORMS OF INCENTIVE

1. Investment grants

The maximum grant available in the Atlantic region is 25% of the capital costs plus 30% of wages and salaries. In the other regions designated for assistance under the legislation the maximum incentive available is 20% of capital costs plus 15% of wages and salaries.

The employment-related component of the incentive **program** is applicable only in the case of new plants or new product expansions. For modernizations and normal expansion, the maximum grants available in all designated regions are 20%.

The upper limit on the size of the development incentive is C$30,000 per job created directly in the facility, or one-half of the capital to be employed in the operation, whichever is the lesser amount.

The incentives are exempt from income tax.

2. Loan guarantees

The Federal Government may guarantee repayment of a loan and interest up to 90% of the advances to manufacturing and processing establishments and certain types of commercial and research facilities, provided that the amount of the loan is less than 80% of the capital cost after deducting the development incentive and all other federal, provincial or municipal grants or other financial assistance it has received or to which it is entitled in connection with the project.

DENMARK

I. COVERAGE OF THE INCENTIVES

Under the 1972 Act on Regional Development the following areas have been designated as development areas: North, West and South Jutland and the islands of Lolland, Falster, Langeland, Faroe, Samsoe and Bornholm. The areas cover 56% of the territory and 30% of the population.

The Faroe Islands have also been designated for assistance under the 1972 Act.

II. MAIN FORMS OF INCENTIVE

1. Investment grants

These are generally only available in areas facing special difficulties for investment purposes in industrial and service enterprises to a maximum of 25%. The grant is taxable.

2. Assistance towards working costs

Working capital grants are available to firms, which have had substantially reduced working results caused by the location in an industrially less developed area.

3. Grants for moving costs

Grants to cover the cost of moving industrial or service enterprises into a development area from other parts of the country are also available. The moving expenses of key personnel may also be covered.

4.   Loans

These may be given to industrial and service establishments for investment purposes and may cover up to 90% of the cost of building, machinery and equipment, after deduction of maximum allowable mortgage loans and any investment grants, with the possibility of a 5 year repayment-free period. The loans are given at lower than market rate (currently 7.5% p.a. compared with a market rate of between 10% and 11%).

5.   Loan guarantees

State guarantees for loans to provide working capital may be granted to industrial enterprises for a maximum period of 5 years.

6.   Loans to municipalities for factory building

These are granted to municipalities for **factory** building for sale or lease. Loans are given at lower than market rates for a maximum period of 30 years.

FINLAND

I.   COVERAGE OF THE INCENTIVES

The development regions, which are divided into two zones according to the degree of underdevelopment, cover 77% of the area and 46% of the population.

II.   MAIN FORMS OF INCENTIVES

1.   Tax concessions

Free depreciation during 10 years on investments in development areas. When the establishment, expansion or renovation of an industrial enterprise takes place in Zone 1 (the least developed) the taxpayer may for a period of 10 years deduct a further 3% per year of the purchase price of the working assets used in the project.

Fixed assets purchased for establishment, expansion or renewal of the enterprise are not counted as property in either income or property taxation for a period of 10 years following their acquisition.

153

2. Interest subsidies

In Zone 1 the credit for which interest subsidies may be given may attain 60% of the total cost of buildings and other assets. The subsidy on the interest charged by the credit institution is 100% for the first two years and 50% for a further two years. In Zone II the limit on the credit is 50% and the subsidy is 80% of the interest for the first two years and 40% for a further two years.

3. Assistance for municipal factory building

Since March 1971 interest rate subsidies have been available to municipalities in development areas for factory building. The rate of interest is 5% in Zone 1 and 6% in Zone II.

4. Regional development fund

This is a credit company, the majority of whose shares are State owned. Its main purposes are to increase the supply of capital through loans or share purchase primarily in small and medium-sized firms and, secondly, to promote R and D. The Fund cannot provide more than 75% of the total value of an investment project. Loans are given at market rates.

5. Training programmes

In development areas where there is a shortage of capacity at formal vocational training establishments, special basic vocational training or continued training is available. Participants receive a wage equivalent in addition to unemployment benefit and reimbursement of travel cost.

6. Building of industrial estates

According to the decision of the Government the building of seven industrial estates has been started in the development areas. The public sector participates in the financing mainly through the communes and through the Regional Development Fund.

7. Transport subsidies

Transport subsidies were introduced in 1973 in order to reduce costs in long-distance transport of industrial products from the development areas. The support covers goods traffic by rail and also, with some limitations, transport by sea, air and road. The transport distance has to be more than 266 km and in the case of transport by rail linked with sea transport of at least 100 km. The subsidy varies between 5% and 40% of the freight charged. For transport by sea the subsidy is 1.25 - 5.00 Fmk/ton. For air freight the subsidy is up to 35% of the freight charged.

8. Support to compensate the employment of inexperienced labour

Support is provided from 1973 to firms to compensate the employment of inexperienced labour in the development areas. The maximum support in Zone I is 15,000 Fmk per worker and in Zone II 6,000 Fmk per worker. A maximum of 1/3 of this support is in the form of a grant and the remainder in the form of a 15 year loan, of which 5 years are free from the annual interest of 7%.

FRANCE

I. COVERAGE OF THE INCENTIVES

The aid areas cover the west, south-west, the Massif Central, Corsica and the mining areas in the North, Lorraine, Central France and the South. They cover 44% of the land area and 36% of the population.

II. MAIN FORMS OF INCENTIVES

1. Investment grants

The maximum grant for investment purposes ranges from 12% to 25% depending on the area. In all areas grants are limited to 15,000 Frs per job created in the case of new installations and to 12,000 Frs for expansion.

2. Loans

These are given exceptionally by the FDES for encouraging industrial decentralization and reconstruction schemes. These can cover about one third of the investment. The rate of interest is at present about 6.75%, i.e. about 2 points below market rate.

155

3.   Participation in enterprise capital

Regional development companies may participate in the capital of enterprises to a limit of 35% for a maximum of 15 years.

4.   Decentralization incentives

i)   A grant covering about 60% of the removal cost incurred by companies moving out of the Paris region or of the 5 cantons south of the Oise is allotted provided at least 500 sq. m. of industrial building space is vacated.

ii)   Decentralization allowances reaching 10, 15 or 20% of investments according to the nature of the activity are also available for tertiary activities transferred from the Paris region. Allowances are limited to 15,000 Frs per job created.

iii)   Partial refund of vocational training costs incurred by companies which set up or move to the provinces; aids for training and re-training; refund of removal and resettling of personnel.

iv)   The authorities may intervene to bring down the cost of land, according to the case, to 10 Frs per sq. m. or 6 Frs per sq. m. in the West, figures which compare with averages of between 15 and 25 Frs per sq. m. in industrial areas.

v)   Certain discounts on the cost of energy may be given, e.g. natural gas in the south-west, electricity in Brittany.

5.   Fiscal aids

The following cumulative but not automatic advantages may be given:

- exceptional amortization of 25% of the cost of buildings in the first year while normally it is 5%;

- partial or total exoneration of the "patente" for a maximum period of 5 years provided that the local authorities have voted for exoneration;

- reduction from 10% to 5% of the tax due on the capital gain derived from the sale of developable land;

- reduction of the transfer tax.

FEDERAL REPUBLIC OF GERMANY

I. COVERAGE OF THE INCENTIVES

Regional Action Programmes have been drawn up for 21 regions within which 312 development areas have been designated. Very broadly, the designated regions cover the Saar, the Belgian and Dutch border areas, the north, parts of Bavaria, Franconia and the Eastern border areas. These cover 58% of the land area and 33% of the population.

II. MAIN FORMS OF INCENTIVES

1. Investment grants

A graduated system of investment grants depending on the category of development area is used. The grant ranges from 10% to 25% to a maximum of DM 100 million per project.

2. Loans

Long-term loans are available from two sources:

- the unemployment insurance fund (BAVAV) provides 10 year loans with 2 years free of redemption at 3.5%. These loans may not exceed DM 1 million nor 10% of the investment;

- the ERP fund provides 20 year loans at 6%. These may not exceed 30% of the investment.

(The amount of interest subsidy can only be cumulated with a grant to the extent of the maximum grant allowable for the area.)

3. Loan guarantees

These are given to the extent of 90% of a loan and to a maximum of 5 million DM.

4. Assistance for manpower training

The State reimburses wages and social charges during the training period, in general for 10 to 30 weeks according to the craft.

5. Special aids in the Eastern border areas

- Freight subsidies for firms faced with additional freight charges arising from the severance of previous economic links with the East.

- Special depreciation allowances of up to 50% on movable assets and 30% for fixed assets.

- Priority in Government contract awards.

GREECE

I. COVERAGE OF THE INCENTIVES

The incentives apply to the provinces outside the Greater Athens area. (The latter accounts for 29% of the population (1971) and 47% of industrial employment (1969).)

II. MAIN FORMS OF INCENTIVES

The incentives to provincial industry under various legislation, especially Law 147/67 as modified and improved by Law 607/68, consist of tax reliefs, high depreciation allowances, exemptions from employers' social security contributions, leniency in certain aspects of tax administration, exemption from duty on capital goods imports, etc. Licensing of new industrial building provides an additional tool for influencing industrial location as do Government Procurement policies.

IRELAND

I. COVERAGE OF THE INCENTIVES

The system of incentives covers the whole country with special provisions for the designated areas. These are mainly the twelve counties in the West and cover 56% of the land area and 31% of the population.

II.   MAIN FORMS OF INCENTIVES

1.   Investment grants

    a)   New industry

    -    A basic grant of up to 40% of the cost of fixed assets for new industrial undertakings satisfying certain conditions.   The limit of 40% applies only to the designated areas.   In the rest of the country, the limit is 25%.

    -    An additional grant of up to 20% determined by reference to the significance and character of the employment likely to be provided, the development or utilization of local materials, the potentiality of linkages with existing firms or potential new enterprises, the technological or scientific content or the existence of exceptional growth potential.

    In practice the following maximum grant rates are now applied by the IDA for projects where the investment does not exceed £1 million; for many projects grants are given at less than these rates.

| AREA | THE MAXIMUM GRANT OBTAINABLE IS THE LESSER OF: | |
	% OF THE COST OF FIXED ASSETS	£ PER PREDICTED JOB AT FULL PRODUCTION
Designated areas	50	5,000
Non-designated areas apart from Dublin	35	4,000
Dublin	25	3,000

    b)   Small industries*

    A grant of up to 60% of the cost of fixed assets in the designated areas.   The corresponding maximum for non-designated areas is 45%.

    *   A small industry is defined, in the designated areas, as an enterprise employing not more than 50 people and with fixed assets not exceeding £100,000: outside the designated areas the comparable figures are 30 people and £60,000.

(Save in exceptional cases, these grants are not payable in the Dublin area and in these exceptional cases, the maximum grant available is 35% of fixed assets).

c) Re-equipment

Grants towards the cost of re-equipment, modernization improvement or extension of industrial undertakings can amount to 35% of investment in the designated areas and 25% elsewhere.

2. Interest rebates and guarantees

Under the Industrial Development Act, 1969, the IDA is empowered to make grants towards the reduction of interest charges on loans for fixed investment secured by industries satisfying the requisite conditions. The IDA may also guarantee the repayment of loans for industrial investment. To date, little use has been made of these powers.

3. Training grants

Training grants may be made by the IDA towards the cost of training workers in industrial undertakings satisfying the necessary conditions.

4. Tax concessions

- Tax exemption on profits for exports of manufactured goods during a 15-year period and partial exemption thereafter until 1990.

- Full relief from import duties on imported plant and machinery.

- 100% depreciation of plant and machinery in the first year and an investment allowance in designated areas of 20%, permitting 120% write-off for tax purposes in the first year.

- Reductions in land and building taxes and on taxes on investment in equipment. In the designated areas local authorities may grant remission for up to ten years of two-thirds of the rates (local taxation) payable on industrial premises.

5. Land and housing

- Provision of low-cost factories and sites in certain areas.

160

- Assistance for the provision of housing for key personnel.

6. Shareholding

The IDA is authorized to take up a share participation in the capital of a firm. This possibility has only been applied in the case of two or three projects of major importance.

ITALY

I. COVERAGE OF THE INCENTIVES

Apart from some areas in the north and centre to which limited measures apply, regional aids apply to the Mezzogiorno. This area covers 38% of the land area and 35% of the population. (The total area covered by assistance measures comprises 50% of the population).

II. MAIN FORMS OF INCENTIVES

1. Investment grants

Depending on the size, the sector and the location, the contribution to capital can vary from a minimum of 7% to a maximum of 50% of the fixed investment.

2. Loans

Financing at reduced rates can vary according to size, sector and location from a minimum of 35% to a maximum of 50% of the fixed investment and for materials upto 40% of the investment itself. The maximum duration of the financial assistance is for 15 years for new undertakings and for 10 years for extensions. The rate of interest varies from a minimum of 3% for small enterprises to a maximum of 6% for the large.

3. Tax concessions

A 10-year exemption on profits tax is accorded. Other fiscal advantages are also accorded.

4. Reduction of social security charges

An allowance of 30% is made on social security charges.

5. Transport concessions

Reductions on rail tariffs for transport of equipment to the Mezzogiorno and for transport of finished products out of the Mezzogiorno. This measure, which would reduce freight charges by 10 to 50% according to the product and the distance involved, has only been applied to a limited extent because of budgetary constraints.

6. Preferential treatment in the award of government contracts

The administration, public enterprises and enterprises with State participation are obliged to reserve 30% of their supply contracts to enterprises in the Mezzogiorno. (At least 40% of investment by public authorities and 80% of investment by companies with State participation must be made in the Mezzogiorno).

JAPAN

I. COVERAGE OF THE INCENTIVES

The 1972 Industrial Relocation Promotion Law incorporates the two major concepts of Departure Promotion Areas for industries which are already overcrowded and should expel some industry and of Relocation Reception Areas for regions which should attract new industry. Departure Promotion areas are the Tokyo and Kinki regions while the Relocation Reception Areas cover the whole of Hokkaido, Tohoku, Hokuriki, San'in, Shihoku, Kyusho and Okinawa as well as a few other prefectures and their adjacent towns and villages.

II. MAIN FORMS OF INCENTIVES

1. Loans or purchasing in connection with the former site of the relocating industry

The Industrial Relocation and Coal Mining Development Corporation provides loans using the old site as collateral for the period beginning from the time the decision is taken to move and ending with the actual

sale, provided that the old sites are used so as to improve the environment and that due consideration is given to environmental protection
in the area into which the plants are moved. While there is no limit
to the total loan amount available in each case, the maximum collateral
value of the site is set at 80% of its estimated market value at a 7.5%
rate of interest with a three year repayment period. This loan can be
used in combination with a regional development loan or a local
dispersion loan from the Japan Development Bank. If a relocating
company cannot make an adequate sale of its old site, the Corporation
purchases the site at current market value and then resells it to those
who will use it in such a way as to improve the environment. In this
case priority is given to central and local governments and their
agencies.

2. Loans for removal expenses

The Corporation may make loans at 8% p. a. for three years to
cover upto 50% of the removal cost of equipment.

3. Grants for relocating industries

Grants to the order of 5,000 yen per sq. m. of the outgoing or
incoming factories are available to local governments and communities
in order to defray the costs of welfare facilities and environmental
protection facilities in the vicinity. As far as the grants are concerned most of them are directed to improving the environment and welfare
of the local communities involved.

4. Fiscal concessions

A system of accelerated depreciation applies to buildings and
equipment of factories moving out of Departure Promotion Areas.
Various other fiscal concessions such as reductions on local taxes
(compensated for by the Central Government) are also available.

5. Assistance for factory building

The Central Government provides interest assistance funds when
industrial parks are built by local governments or by development
corporations to ensure that the interest burden does not exceed 6.5%
p. a. For rates above this level assistance upto 1.7 percentage
points of the interest rate incurred can be covered by the Government.
The corporation may construct industrial parks in selected areas.

NETHERLANDS

I. COVERAGE OF THE INCENTIVES

Two areas have been designated for stimulation: the Northern development area and South Limburg. The new town of Lelystad also benefits from certain measures. These areas cover 30% of the land area and 17% of the population.

II. MAIN FORMS OF INCENTIVES

1. Investment grants

For new industrial establishments investment grants amounting to 25% of the acquisition cost of fixed assets (machinery, buildings, land) are available subject to a maximum of Gld. 3 million. For industrial extensions the grant is reduced to 15% and to a maximum of Gld. 1.8 million. The Minister of Economic Affairs however can decide to exceed the maximum whenever he feels this to be justified by particular circumstances. To qualify, in the case of new acquisitions, the investment must be at least Gld. 400 thousand and, in the case of extensions, at least Gld. 500 thousand.

In the service sector a grant of 25% to a maximum of Gld. 3 million is available on investments of at least Gld. 400 thousand. To qualify, an enterprise must serve more than just local markets.

2. Loan guarantees

State guarantees for loans from the Nationale Investeringsbank. These loans are given at market rates for a maximum of 15 years with, in some cases, 5 years free of redemption.

3. Interest subsidies

This possibility, although available, has not yet received practical application (up to 3% p. a. over a maximum period of 15 years of capital financing investment).

4. Shareholding

Part of a capital of a firm may be subscribed to by the Nationale Investeringsbank or other financial institutions with State guarantees of

164

a minimum dividend for a limited period. In certain circumstances the State may participate directly in the capital. In order to further the socio-economic development of the Northern Stimulation Area the Minister of Economic Affairs set up the Northern Development Company Ltd **early** in 1974. This body will have the possibility of participating - with Government funds - in new establishments, in existing enterprises or may set up new firms by itself.

5. Tax concessions

Accelerated depreciation on one third of the buildings acquired and the possibility of offsetting losses during the first six years against later profits for an unlimited period.

6. Training grants

The State contributes in some cases towards the cost of training labour.

7. Assistance for labour mobility

In the spring of 1973 the system for assisting labour moving from the west to other parts of the country was enlarged with a stronger incentive for movements towards the north.

NORWAY

I. COVERAGE OF THE INCENTIVES TO ENTERPRISES

It is up to the Regional Development Fund (RDF) to delimit the areas eligible for assistance. About 45% of the population live in areas in which enterprises at present may get support from the RDF.

II. MAIN FORMS OF INCENTIVES

1. Loans and loan guarantees

The RDF provides long and medium term loans and guarantees for investment purposes at market rates and fairly liberal terms, for "top financing" of investments.

2. Relocation grants

This incentive applies to enterprises which transfer their activities
from a developed to a less developed district. Grants may cover
expenses involved in the moving of machinery and equipment, transfer
of staff and losses caused by interruption of production.

3. Manpower training grants

Such assistance applies to the starting up of new enterprises as
well as to relocation. It may include wages, travelling, board and
lodging expenses for instructors or key personnel as well as 50% of
wages for workers up to a three-month period.

4. Investment grants

Since 1971 an investment grant of up to 35% is available in North-
Norway and in one county on the west coast, up to 25% in some other
designated areas, and up to 15% in the rest of the areas confronted
with some employment problems or weak economic bases.

5. Tax concessions

Tax free deductions for the purpose of investment in development
districts may generally be made up to 25% of taxable income, or up to
50% provided that taxable income is not in this way brought below the
average of the last two years.

6. Transport compensation grants

Grants up to 40% may be given towards transport costs incurred
by manufacturers in the north and in mid-west coastal areas with the
proviso that the minimum transport distance is 300 km.

7. Provision of factory buildings

A Norwegian version of the British system of industrial estates
was initiated in 1968. In 1968-69 five small centres were selected for
the location of state-owned industrial land and buildings for sale or
lease. Since then 5 additional places have been selected (of which 3 in
1973-74). Municipalities have adopted a similar system financed
partly by the Regional Development Fund.

8. Industrial location service

By an act of 1970 an advisory location service combined with a compulsory notification system was established. Industrial firms in some specified "pressure" areas have to give advance notice to the advisory location agency about their intentions to build premises for major expansion or new plants within these areas. The board of the advisory agency has the duty to consider alternative locations and give advise to the firm.

SPAIN

I. COVERAGE OF THE INCENTIVES

They apply to firms setting up or expanding in the industrial promotion poles and industrial development poles and in the industrial zones in rural areas. In 1967, the population in the seven industrial poles represented approximately 6% of the total population.

II. MAIN FORMS OF THE INCENTIVES

1. Investment grants

A maximum grant of 20% on fixed investments is available in the case of the promotion poles and of 10% in the development poles.

2. Loans

Preference is given for obtaining official credit in the absence of other sources of finance. In general it is provided at lower rates and for longer periods than from other sources.

3. Tax concessions

Important fiscal reductions, going up to 95% and exemptions on taxes bearing on the creation of new enterprises and on the importation of machinery and equipment from abroad where this is not produced in Spain. Free depreciation is possible during the first five years.

SWEDEN

I. COVERAGE OF THE INCENTIVES

For purposes of regional development there is a General Aid Area covering two-thirds of the total area and less than 20% of the population of the whole country and within this an Inner Aid Area covering half of the total area and some 5% of the population of the whole country. In special circumstances when considerable employment difficulties are expected to arise, assistance may be given to other parts of the country.

II. MAIN FORMS OF INCENTIVES

1. Investment grants

Grants are payable in connection with the construction, extension or conversion of premises. These normally amount to a maximum of 50% of the costs of building investments. As of 1st July, 1973, grants in the Inner Aid Area, in exceptional circumstances, can be increased to 65% and be made available for investment in machinery and tools as well.

2. Loans

Location loans, which are payable in respect of investment in buildings, machinery and tools, may not, taken together with grants, exceed two-thirds of the total investment cost. Under special circumstances loans may be interest-free for a maximum of 3 years and a maximum of 5 years free of redemption.

3. Loan guarantees

Government guarantees may be given to financial institutions for loans to enterprises for working capital.

4. Refunds for removal costs

These are payable to enterprises which move their activity to a locality within the General Aid area.

5. Training grants

In conjunction with setting up or expanding activity within the General Aid area, a training grant is payable for a period of 6 months at the rate of 5 S. Kr. per hour for each new employee. In special cases the grant may be paid over a longer period and at a higher rate.

6. Employment grants

Employment grants were introduced in 1970 and so far during a trial period have been granted only to industrial undertakings in the Inner Aid Area. This support has been made a regular measure as from July 1, 1973, and is now available for largely the same category of firms that are entitled to location aid.

Employment grants are available solely in the Inner Aid Area and only for increases in employment. As from July 1st, 1973, the grant for the first year is Skr 7,000 for each additional employee. If the increase is maintained, a grant is paid for a second year with another Skr 7,000 and for a third year with Skr 3,500, totalling Skr 17,500.

7. Investment reserve funds

Under this system, joint-stock companies and certain other enterprises may set aside a maximum of 40% of pre-tax annual profits in an investment fund, provided that part of it (40-46%) be paid into an account at the Bank of Sweden which bears no interest. The entreprise may then be given special permission to use a certain portion of its fund for investment purposes, i. e. to further the aims of regional policy.

If so, the book value of the investment is considered to have been reduced by an equivalent amount. Instead, the enterprise is entitled to an extra pre-tax deduction amounting to 10% of the fund assets used.

Thus, the use of the investment funds involves considerable tax subsidies.

8. Transport subsidies

Transport subsidies connected with regional policy were introduced in 1971 in order to offset the disadvantageous costs inherent in long-distance transport from the General Aid Area.

Following a Parliament resolution in the spring of 1973, regional transport subsidies have been increased with effect from January 1, 1974. Briefly the new rules are as follows.

Subsidies are payable in the first instance for transport of goods by road and rail in the General Aid Area over distances exceeding 250 km (which also includes any constituent mileage on Finnish or Norwegian territory). A further requirement is for the goods concerned to have undergone some form of processing in the area.

Among other things, the new rules imply that transport subsidies have been extended to include types of transport into the General Aid Area from elsewhere in Sweden involving raw materials and semi-manufactured products destined to be worked up in the area. To avoid negative effects on sales of such products originating in the area, subsidies for incoming transport have been restricted to firms in certain industries and do not apply e. g. to the timber and pulp industry, the wood processing industry and the building materials industry.

Transport subsidies vary between 15 and 35% of the freight charged, depending on the distance involved and the location of the consigner. The maximum rate applies to transport over distances of 500 km or more.

UNITED KINGDOM

I. COVERAGE OF THE INCENTIVES

Regional measures are based on a structure of priority areas: Great Britain.

i) Development Areas. Originally designated in 1966, these cover most of Scotland, Wales and the Northern region of England, Merseyside and parts of the South-West. They cover approximately 54% of the total land area and 21% of total employees (self-employed are excluded).

ii) Special Development Areas. Originally designated in 1967, to take account of particularly serious problems arising from the decline of coal mining, they were extended in 1971 to cover some other old industrial centres suffering from severe sectoral industrial problems. They are all within the Development Areas, in Scotland, Wales and the Northern region and cover 8. 6% of total employees.

170

iii)   Intermediate Areas. These areas which receive only a part
of the regional assistance were first established in 1970 and then
enlarged in 1971 and 1972. They provide approximately 21% of total
employees.

Development Areas and Intermediate Areas together account for
65% of the land area of Great Britain and for 42% of all employees. In
addition there is a Derelict Land Clearance Area which receives
preferential grants for the clearance of industrially derelict land.
Incentives similar in kind to those offered in Development Areas are
available to firms in Northern Ireland, but they are offered under
separate powers and are administered by the Government of Northern
Ireland.

II.   MAIN FORMS OF INCENTIVES IN GREAT BRITAIN

1.   Regional development grants

A 20% grant (22% in special development areas) for investment
in plant, new, machinery and industrial buildings in development areas.
Grants at 20% for industrial buildings only in intermediate areas,
and for 2 years in the North Midlands derelict land clearance area.
These grants are free of tax.

2.   Selective financial assistance

This is available for projects including certain service projects
which are likely to provide, maintain and safeguard employment in the
assisted areas. It may be given in various forms: loans, grants in
relief of interest or purchase of shares. The normal forms of
assistance are loans at below market rates when additional employment
is created. In other cases the rate is approximately the commercial
one. As from June 1973 certain mobile service projects may be given
up to £800 for each employee moved with his work up to a limit of
50% of the number of additional jobs created in an assisted area; plus
the rent of premises at the new location for up to 5 years in Development Areas and 3 years in Intermediate Areas.

3.   Creation of industrial estates and factory construction

The three Industrial Estate Corporations equip sites and construct
factories for sale or rent at market value. For manufacturing projects
providing additional jobs rent may in certain circumstances be waived
for two years.

4. Regional employment premium

This was introduced in 1967. It amounts to £1.5 per full-time adult male employee per week and £0.75 per adult female employee in manufacturing undertakings in the development and special development areas.

5. Training grants

Grants to industry for training workers for additional jobs in assisted areas (£15 per week in respect of each man with lower rates for women and young persons).

6. Transfer grants

Grants for the transfer of industrial undertakings to assisted areas under the Selective Assistance arrangements referred to above. These may amount to 80% of certain costs of transfer.

7. Removal and rehousing grants

Certain payments may be made towards the removal and installation costs of workers regarded as essential to start up new undertakings in assisted areas.

8. Preferential contract awards

A degree of preference is given in public sector contracts to undertakings in the Development Areas and Special Development Areas, but not involving any price preference.

9. Tax concessions

Regional Development Grants are not treated as reducing capital expenditure for the purpose of calculating tax allowances. In other respects there is no difference between the tax treatment of the various parts of Great Britain.

OECD SALES AGENTS
DEPOSITAIRES DES PUBLICATIONS DE L'OCDE

ARGENTINA – ARGENTINE
Carlos Hirsch S.R.L.,
Florida 165, BUENOS-AIRES.
☎ 33-1787-2391 Y 30-7122

AUSTRALIA – AUSTRALIE
B.C.N. Agencies Pty, Ltd.,
161 Sturt St., South MELBOURNE, Vic. 3205.
☎ 69.7601
658 Pittwater Road, BROOKVALE NSW 2100.
☎ 938 2267

AUSTRIA – AUTRICHE
Gerold and Co., Graben 31, WIEN 1.
☎ 52.22.35

BELGIUM – BELGIQUE
Librairie des Sciences
Coudenberg 76-78, B 1000 BRUXELLES 1.
☎ 13.37.36/12.05.60

BRAZIL – BRESIL
Mestre Jou S.A., Rua Guaipá 518,
Caixa Postal 24090, 05089 SAO PAULO 10.
☎ 256-2746/262-1609
Rua Senador Dantas 19 s/205-6, RIO DE
JANEIRO GB. ☎ 232-07. 32

CANADA
Information Canada
171 Slater, OTTAWA. K1A 0S9.
☎ (613) 992-9738

DENMARK – DANEMARK
Munksgaards Boghandel
Nørregade 6, 1165 KØBENHAVN K.
☎ (01) 12 69 70

FINLAND – FINLANDE
Akateeminen Kirjakauppa
Keskuskatu 1, 00100 HELSINKI 10. ☎ 625.901

FRANCE
Bureau des Publications de l'OCDE
2 rue André-Pascal, 75775 PARIS CEDEX 16.
☎ 524.81.67
Principaux correspondants :
13602 AIX-EN-PROVENCE : Librairie de
l'Université. ☎ 26.18.08
38000 GRENOBLE : B. Arthaud. ☎ 87.25.11
31000 TOULOUSE : Privat. ☎ 21.09.26

GERMANY – ALLEMAGNE
Verlag Weltarchiv G.m.b.H.
D 2000 HAMBURG 36, Neuer Jungfernstieg 21
☎ 040-35-62-501

GREECE – GRECE
Librairie Kauffmann, 28 rue du Stade,
ATHENES 132. ☎ 322.21.60

ICELAND – ISLANDE
Snaebjörn Jónsson and Co., h.f.,
Hafnarstræti 4 and 9, P.O.B. 1131,
REYKJAVIK. ☎ 13133/14281/11936

INDIA – INDE
Oxford Book and Stationery Co. :
NEW DELHI, Scindia House. ☎ 47388
CALCUTTA, 17 Park Street. ☎ 24083

IRELAND – IRLANDE
Eason and Son, 40 Lower O'Connell Street,
P.O.B. 42, DUBLIN 1. ☎ 01-41161

ISRAEL
Emanuel Brown :
35 Allenby Road, TEL AVIV. ☎ 51049/54082
also at :
9, Shlomzion Hamalka Street, JERUSALEM.
☎ 234807
48 Nahlath Benjamin Street, TEL AVIV.
☎ 53276

ITALY – ITALIE
Libreria Commissionaria Sansoni :
Via Lamarmora 45, 50121 FIRENZE. ☎ 579751
Via Bartolini 29, 20155 MILANO. ☎ 365083
Sous-dépositaires :
Editrice e Libreria Herder,
Piazza Montecitorio 120, 00186 ROMA.
☎ 674628
Libreria Hoepli, Via Hoepli 5, 20121 MILANO.
☎ 865446
Libreria Lattes, Via Garibaldi 3, 10122 TORINO.
☎ 519274
La diffusione delle edizioni OCDE è inoltre assicu-
rata dalle migliori librerie nelle città più importanti.

JAPAN – JAPON
OECD Publications Centre,
Akasaka Park Building,
2-3-4 Akasaka,
Minato-ku
TOKYO 107. ☎ 586-2016
Maruzen Company Ltd.,
6 Tori-Nichome Nihonbashi, TOKYO 103,
P.O.B. 5050, Tokyo International 100-31.
☎ 272-7211

LEBANON – LIBAN
Documenta Scientifica/Redico
Edison Building, Bliss Street,
P.O.Box 5641, BEIRUT. ☎ 354429 – 344425

THE NETHERLANDS – PAYS-BAS
W.P. Van Stockum
Buitenhof 36, DEN HAAG. ☎ 070-65.68.08

NEW ZEALAND – NOUVELLE-ZELANDE
The Publications Officer
Government Printing Office
Mulgrave Street (Private Bag)
WELLINGTON, ☎ 46.807
and Government Bookshops at
AUCKLAND (P.O.B. 5344). ☎ 32.919
CHRISTCHURCH (P.O.B. 1721). ☎ 50.331
HAMILTON (P.O.B. 857). ☎ 80.103
DUNEDIN (P.O.B. 1104). ☎ 78.294

NORWAY – NORVEGE
Johan Grundt Tanums Bokhandel,
Karl Johansgate 41/43, OSLO 1. ☎ 02-332980

PAKISTAN
Mirza Book Agency, 65 Shahrah Quaid-E-Azam,
LAHORE 3. ☎ 66839

PHILIPPINES
R.M. Garcia Publishing House,
903 Quezon Blvd. Ext., QUEZON CITY,
P.O. Box 1860 – MANILA. ☎ 99.98.47

PORTUGAL
Livraria Portugal,
Rua do Carmo 70-74. LISBOA 2. ☎ 360582/3

SPAIN – ESPAGNE
Libreria Mundi Prensa
Castelló 37, MADRID-1. ☎ 275.46.55
Libreria Bastinos
Pelayo, 52, BARCELONA 1. ☎ 222.06.00

SWEDEN – SUEDE
Fritzes Kungl. Hovbokhandel,
Fredsgatan 2, 11152 STOCKHOLM 16.
☎ 08/23 89 00

SWITZERLAND – SUISSE
Librairie Payot, 6 rue Grenus, 1211 GENEVE 11.
☎ 022-31.89.50

TAIWAN
Books and Scientific Supplies Services, Ltd.
P.O.B. 83, TAIPEI.

TURKEY – TURQUIE
Librairie Hachette,
469 Istiklal Caddesi,
Beyoglu, ISTANBUL, ☎ 44.94.70
et 14 E Ziya Gökalp Caddesi
ANKARA. ☎ 12.10.80

UNITED KINGDOM – ROYAUME-UNI
H.M. Stationery Office, P.O.B. 569, LONDON
SE1 9 NH, ☎ 01-928-6977, Ext. 410
or
49 High Holborn
LONDON WC1V 6HB (personal callers)
Branches at: EDINBURGH, BIRMINGHAM,
BRISTOL, MANCHESTER, CARDIFF,
BELFAST.

UNITED STATES OF AMERICA
OECD Publications Center, Suite 1207,
1750 Pennsylvania Ave, N.W.
WASHINGTON, D.C. 20006. ☎ (202)298-8755

VENEZUELA
Libreria del Este, Avda. F. Miranda 52,
Edificio Galipán, Aptdo. 60 337, CARACAS 106.
☎ 32 23 01/33 26 04/33 24 73

YUGOSLAVIA – YOUGOSLAVIE
Jugoslovenska Knjiga, Terazije 27, P.O.B. 36,
BEOGRAD. ☎ 621-992

Les commandes provenant de pays ou l'OCDE n'a pas encore désigné de dépositaire
peuvent être adressées à :
OCDE, Bureau des Publications, 2 rue André-Pascal, 75775 Paris CEDEX 16
Orders and inquiries from countries where sales agents have not yet been appointed may be sent to
OECD, Publications Office, 2 rue André-Pascal, 75775 Paris CEDEX 16

OECD PUBLICATIONS, 2, rue André-Pascal, 75775 Paris Cedex 16 - No. 33657 - 1974

PRINTED IN FRANCE